ENDORSEMENTS

"Dave's book resonates with easy to read ideas with simplified methods for follow through. This book is recommended reading for those who aspire to move their careers forward. Corporate executives or entrepreneurs will benefit equally. This book should be in every business library."—Nido Qubein, Chairman, Great Harvest Bread Company, President, High Point University.

Dave Yoho has helped millions to have great years through his speaking. In this book he has given us the wisdom of a life time to read, re-read and share. Thank you Dave.—Charles A. "Tremendous" Jones, author, *Life is Tremendous*

"Whether you are in the military, government or private industry, the complex issues which face our society may seem overwhelming. Dave Yoho's EPOD Theory is applicable for almost everyone. Having known, admired and respected Dave for almost 30 years, I promise you will be enriched by the ideas in his book and will be better prepared to face the challenges of tomorrow."—Brig. General Steve Ritchie, USAF, (Ret.).

"On the playing field of life, great wisdom is gathered by examining the history of others. This book contains not only practical advice but ideas and principles by which to live your life. It's what makes leaders and legends."—Jim Tunney, NFL Referee (Ret.).

"Dave deals with facts not fiction. His case studies are compact and easy to understand. His ideas will aid you in your business or personal plan, and in a time when there is such pervasive negativity, this book is a beacon for positivity."—David L. Moore, Chairman, Sonostar Ventures, LLC.

"Dave is a masterful orator, wise businessman and mentor to millions. He has produced a simple to understand study for those in search of greatness. This is a masterfully crafted, power packed book."—Naomi Rhode, CPAE, Past President, National Speakers Assn., Global President, International Federation of Professional Speakers.

"In an ever growing world of complex issues and changes, Dave Yoho provides a masterful use of business and personal ideas which will benefit readers at any stage of life or career."—Dr. L. Bevel Jones, United Methodist Bishop (Ret.).

"I've watched him work his magic on live audiences and on video. His in depth knowledge of human behavior and business lore kept him at the top of his profession. Now he makes this wisdom available in *Have A Great Year Every Year*. I've been a Dave Yoho student for nearly four decades—never disappointed. Get the book."—Ty Boyd, Chairman, Executive Learning Systems.

Dave Yoho: Presides over one of the oldest and most successful consulting groups in the U.S.—He sits on the board of public companies, has appeared in over 100 video training series and has made over 5,000 speeches.

HAVE A GREAT
YEAR EVERY YEAR

Dave Yoho

HAVE A GREAT YEAR EVERY YEAR

A Four Point Program for Maximizing Your Performance

Dave Yoho

OAKHILL PRESS
Winchester, VA

© 2005 Dave Yoho

All rights reserved.

Reproduction or translation of any part of this work beyond that permitted by Section 107 or 108 of the 1976 United States Copyright Act without the permission of the copyright owner is unlawful. Requests for permission or further information should be addressed to the Permissions Department, Oakhill Press.

This publication is designed to provide accurate and authoritative information in regard to the subject matter covered. It is sold with the understanding that the publisher is not engaged in rendering legal, accounting, or other professional service. If legal advice or other expert assistance is required, the services of a competent professional person should be sought. *From a Declaration of Principles jointly adopted by a committee of the American Bar Association and a committee of publishers.*

Without limiting the rights under copyright reserved above, no part of this publication may be reproduced, stored in or introduced into a retrieval system, or transmitted, in any form or by any means (electronic, mechanical, photocopying, recording or otherwise) without the prior written permission of the publisher of this book.

10 9 8 7 6 5 4 3 2 1

Book design and production by BookComp, Inc
Jacket Design by Michael Komarck
Printed in the United States of America

Library of Congress Cataloging-in-Publication Data
Yoho, Dave.
   Have a great year every year : the EPOD theory / by Dave Yoho. — [2nd ed.]
      p. cm.
   Rev. ed. of: How to have a good year every year. 1991.
   ISBN 1-886939-69-1
    1. Success in business. 2. Psychology, Industrial. I. Yoho, Dave. How to have a good year every year. II. Title.
HF5386.Y53 2004
650.1—dc22

                                                                             204059979

Oakhill Press
1647 Cedar Grove Road
Winchester, VA 22603
800-32-books
Printed in the United States of America

VOX POPULI

When the first edition of this book, then titled *How to Have a Good Year Every Year*, hit the bookstores in 1991, we were told by the publisher that we had a winner.

Since then, the book has been reprinted in several languages and was popular in England, Australia, and Canada.

We were told the abundance of ideas coupled with the simplicity of reading them made the book an investment that paid immediate dividends for the reader.

Much has changed since 1991. In this new millennium the economy, social interaction, buyer habits, and world events have all undergone radical change. Many of those people featured in the earlier edition have gone to their great reward. However, we were encouraged to rewrite this book with many new case histories and updated formats. We believe you, the reader, will be intrigued by the updated information, new ideas, and case studies.

We were encouraged by our readers, clients, and business associates to produce this new work, now entitled *Have A Great Year Every Year*. We trust you will enjoy it. We also enjoy hearing from our readers, so log on to my Web site *www.daveyoho.com* and send me an email.

ACKNOWLEDGMENTS

My personality, skills, and behavior and are all an outgrowth of my history, life experiences, and those with whom I have interacted.

I appreciate those whose life experiences and business success have been examined for this work.

My teachers, mentors, and supporters gave me their time, for which I am enriched. My clients and business associates shared their personal histories, which enabled me to gain insights not otherwise available.

Thanks to my competent staff for their many contributions. To Betty Carvalho, my administrative assistant for her diligence in retyping my dictation and longhand notes, and to Brad Yoho, who acted as my rewrite editor, I am eternally grateful.

To you, the reader—who may be a friend I have yet to meet—I hope you read within my work something that you do not understand or an idea with which you do not agree. *"The power of an idea can be measured by the degree of resistance it creates."*

To Carole, who saw fit to invest her life in our marriage and without whom life and loving could not have been as it is.

To all I give these words I wrote thirty years ago:

Peace is not a season, it is a way of life.
May it be yours. If you search for the person
You would like to be, you may never get to
*Enjoy the person you are.**

Peace and T.U.A.
Dave Yoho

*Peace Is Not a Season © Copyright Dave Yoho Associates

FOREWORD

by Mark Victor Hansen, coauthor,
Chicken Soup for the Soul series

Millions of dollars and billions of hours have been spent buying and reading books or listening to tapes, the intent of which was to make the reader/listener better informed and thus enabled to develop a life or business plan that ensures some modicum of success.

In my authorship of over seventy-four books, the circulation for which at this writing is over 82 million copies, I have read through thousands of manuscripts, listened to hundreds of proposals, and examined the writings or works of the popular authors of our times. As such, I feel both qualified and compelled to author this introduction to the second edition of *Have A Great Year Every Year*.

This book may appear to contain vignettes and examples about the success stories of others, yet it is so much more. You are given this opportunity to view the world of success through the objective eyes of Dave Yoho, and herein lies the difference with this and many other books you've read in the past. Because Dave Yoho founded a successful multimillion-dollar conglomerate, which he sold when still a very young man; has made over five thousand speeches; represented many of the Fortune 500 companies as a consultant; and sits on the board of public corporations, you are receiving the benefit of his ability to disseminate information, separate fact from fiction, and ultimately describe realistic ways for you to emulate the patterns described in the case histories.

The first edition of *How to Have a Good Year Every Year* (Berkley Press, 1991), was embraced by corporate leaders and everyday citizens of the United States, Canada, and Australia, as well as Japan and China where it was translated into their languages. The point is that, through Dave's eyes, the information has universal appeal to which you, the reader, will soon attest.

Dave has had firsthand working knowledge of the majority of the individuals featured in the book. Thus he was afforded opportunities to observe and participate in the inner workings of the material which he has chronicled herein. Dave's keen ability to work within large organizations while ferreting out the human interest stories makes this book both exciting and replicable to those who read the material.

Dave Yoho's writings are also influenced by the two major educational forces that drive the success of his large consulting business: business management and psychology. He is a board member of a public corporation and a member of that company's audit committee at a time when these complex representations require much more than the general understanding of business issues. Additionally, his ability to foresee issues of the future that affect business decisions have attracted Fortune 500 companies to utilize his skills on an advisory basis.

Now, balance the latter against his experience and understanding of sociological and psychological issues that businesses face every day, and you will see the emergence of the unique personality who is equally at home in the halls of giant corporations and the offices of entrepreneurs. It is through these exposures and experiences that he was given access to the people whose stories, methods of operation, and successful patterns make up the body of this great book.

Most of all, *Have A Great Year Every Year* is dedicated to people issues. It is about people who have accomplished unique goals and many who faced impediments that would appear to be barriers. I trust that your response to reading this book will be similar to mine. I feel uplifted by the potential of humankind. I am inspired by the ingenuity of my fellow men and women, and I stand in awe of those who despite difficult beginnings rose to the top.

The late Dr. Norman Vincent Peale said it better than any book reviewer when the first edition of Dave's book was released: "A great book . . . wise, helpful and provocative . . . It has helped me. I'm sure it will help you, too."

I feel twice blessed since I have read this material and, more importantly, have had the opportunity over the past thirty years to know, befriend, and associate with the author, Dave Yoho.

Dave firmly believes in his EPOD Theory (Energy, Persuasion, Optimism, Discipline), which is the genesis of the material in this book. Moreover, he subscribes to the theory that most individuals and organizations possess some or all of these components to some degree. Throughout the book you will see the case histories divided into headings of each of those components. Having heard Dave speak on this subject many times, I understand both the basis and measurability of the EPOD Theory. You, the reader, are then challenged to measure your own style and practices to determine where you can improve your own contribution to this four-part program, which when applied will aid you in improving your performance.

I know you will find this book a worthwhile addition to your library that you will come back to time and again. I trust that you, like many others, will start to practice and then gain from the implementation of the ideas you will find in here.

Once more, I applaud your choice of this book and encourage you to continue your journey of discovery with this type of reading. I leave you with a phrase that I have often used in my *Chicken Soup for the Soul* series: "The size of your thinking determines the size of your results." Dave Yoho will expand your thinking.

CONTENTS

	Introduction	1
1.	Energy	9
2.	Persuasion: A Vital Element to Your Success	31
3.	Optimism	49
4.	Discipline	69
5.	Create A Power Plan	87
6.	Changing the Rules	101
7.	Selling EPOD Solutions	121
8.	Applying EPOD Theory to Business	147
9.	Movers and Shakers	169
10.	The Power of EPOD Speeches	189
11.	Effective Communication	207
12.	The Human Difference	227
13.	Conclusion	241
	Index	245

INTRODUCTION

The EPOD Theory

"If you can keep your head when all about you are losing theirs and blaming it on you, if you can trust yourself when all men doubt you, yet make allowance for their doubting too . . ."

—*Rudyard Kipling*

We live and operate in an ever-changing world, which in turn makes excessive demands on our need to respond.

Many people spend endless hours searching for a game plan that will respond to their needs and aid them in ultimately meeting their goals.

"How can I be a more effective leader?"

"How can I get consistent productivity and loyalty from my employees and associates?"

"How can I become more competitive and stay profitable?"

"How can I develop, then follow, an effective long-range plan and model for my business?"

"How can I deal with the complex personal challenges in today's society?"

"How can I maintain an optimistic, positive outlook about my career and personal life?"

"How can I improve my interpersonal skills?"

"How can I initiate workable agreements and contracts with a win-win goal?"

"How can I achieve more positive outcomes from my communications?"

As the head of a major consulting group that represents Fortune 500 companies and smaller, closely held businesses, I find most business's problems have more to do with **weaknesses in deployment of human resources** than factors external to the business, and that a business's environment profoundly affects the deployment of human resources.

In this case, "environment" means interaction between individuals or departments, and communication techniques between personnel, customers, and vendors. It includes business policies—how staff, customers, and community are regarded, as well as the physical layout, including lighting, sound, furnishings, and related factors.

Who controls your business or personal environment? You do. And you can control four major elements which contribute to that environment: **Energy, Persuasion, Optimism,** and **Discipline.** The proper application of these elements can serve as the common denominator for all successful individuals and thriving businesses.

Understanding and Using the EPOD Theory

This book enables you to gain an in-depth understanding of how **Energy, Persuasion, Optimism,** and **Discipline** affect your personal life, business, and career. You'll learn how these elements can be properly applied in crucial areas and the keys to thriving regardless of the state of the economy, your level of competition, or the current state of your business.

For years, I sought the answer as to why some businesses and individuals thrived despite obvious limitations, while others blessed with considerable resources did not approach the success one might expect. I also wanted to identify what had led me to prosperity, and what had brought me hardship, pain, and despair, so I could share the lessons with others.

After much examination and research, I was able to view much success through the proper application of the four basic elements that compose the **EPOD Theory.** The EPOD Theory in operating a business, managing a staff, or advancing your career represents the synthesis of my studies in business and psychology, and my forty-plus years as a business owner, consultant, and speaker to both large and small organizations throughout North America, Europe, and Australia.

When I bought into my first company in 1958, the annual sales volume was $350,000. For twenty-two years we averaged 26 percent annual growth (including acquisitions). When I began selling my interests in 1980, the combined annual sales volume was $60 million. Since 1980, I've been a full-time consultant and speaker and have helped thousands of executives, salespeople, and aspiring individuals. By now I've made over five thousand paid speeches and have appeared in over one hundred training movies (videos). I have spoken to audiences in seventeen countries and interviewed thousands of successful individuals.

A Brief Introduction to the Four Elements of EPOD

ENERGY—The energy of an individual or business can be measured by the degree of intensity, enthusiasm, and excitation which is displayed in the interaction between ourselves and others in the transmission of ideas, the buying and selling of products, and the giving and receiving of information.

The opposite of high energy is obviously low energy. The price of low energy is usually determined by the reception we receive from others whom we would like to be responsive to our ideas.

PERSUASION—Persuasion deals mostly with language and verbal skills. It may be one of the least understood of the four elements. When combined with energy, the factor of body language also plays an important role.

How effective are you in getting other people to respond to your ideas; getting the outcomes you want; getting others to buy into new methods, products, and services, to enjoy themselves in their business or personal environment, and to voluntarily spend more time with you?

OPTIMISM—Optimism is an attitude created by a personal decision. The subconscious mind does not know the difference between the real and the imagined. You can imagine yourself healthy, happy, upbeat, and positive, or the opposite.

Optimism enables individuals to thrive in an otherwise negative environment, and by virtue of their optimism become a conduit for change within and to the environment.

DISCIPLINE—Discipline levels can be measured by how frequently and effectively one approaches and completes tasks that he or she doesn't really like to do. Discipline is a commitment to a way of life. It includes the planning of a business or a personal strategy and the routine implementation of that strategy.

Each of the four elements interconnect with one another. In chapter 1 we explore the energy component. In chapters 2, 3, and 4 we continue with persuasion, optimism, and discipline, and discuss their interaction. Then we examine how the EPOD Theory can be applied to the array of situations you face in your business and personal life.

Becoming an EPOD Person

The EPOD Theory is an efficient tool for understanding and internalizing the components of a successful business model. There are also subcomponents to these common denominators. For example, enthusiasm and vigor support high energy. Stamina supports both high energy and discipline, and you can increase your stamina through discipline. The four elements are sufficiently broad and overlap just enough to help explain how success can be achieved using this method.

EPOD elements are not elaborate, exotic, or complex to understand. They are within your grasp each day. While we live in an era in which operating a business is becoming increasingly complicated, the EPOD elements are simple and easy to practice and use.

The EPOD Theory can be applied to all manner of human interaction, and everyone can learn and benefit from it. Whether you are a teenager, senior citizen, or in between, the option of using it is always available. It helps explain why some seniors exhibit more energy than people half their age and some young management types are twice as persuasive as many senior management people. In short, transmitting energy is not as physiological as we are taught to believe.

Be Aware of How You Think and Speak

If you've ever said or thought, "I have no get-up-and-go. Maybe I could have more energy in my life, but I just don't see how," consider the following:

Whatever you are doing right now, you are doing because you would rather be doing it than not be doing it. Whatever you say and whatever you feel are going to affirm how you are. If you say, "I would like to learn how to apply the EPOD elements, but I don't have the time," then you will not have the time.

Though we are surrounded by role models who embody the traits we would like to exhibit, our own language and thoughts can restrict us from the outcomes and goals we would like to achieve. If you see an energetic or charismatic leader and think, *She is impressive, but I could never be like that,* then you never will be. Abundant research has established that it takes a minimum of twenty-one days to substitute a new behavior or practice in place of an old or undesirable one. The next time you encounter someone who inspires you, why not think, *I am going to exhibit more energy.* If this sounds overly simple, try it; make the choice and repeat that statement over and over for twenty-one days. You will find yourself becoming a higher-energy person.

Throughout this book, I'll refer to the twenty-one-day principle in making suggestions for positive change.

Being at Your Best

In private sessions, managers often tell me that they are having a good day or a bad day—a message that I find difficult to understand. The chemicals inside you that can create homeostasis, kinetic energy, or positive feelings don't change that much from day to day. When managers say, "I'm feeling down today," they simply haven't learned that they manufacture the feeling of being up or down. The perception is their option, and ultimately the outcome for most of their day.

How you feel can be influenced by what you are thinking or eating, and even how late you got to bed last night; however, your decision about how you are going to feel ultimately controls the way you will feel.

What Have You Decided about Today?

In the computer industry there is a phrase, GIGO—"Garbage In, Garbage Out"—implying that whatever you put in the computer is what comes out. In behavioral training we often analyze your historical experiences and attitude, then conclude that "Garbage in stays in, unless voluntarily removed." What are you putting into your personal information processor? That today is going to be a great day or a disaster? The chances are whatever you believe, it will be (*qué será será*).

I am frequently asked if I experienced pressure and stress during my complicated travel schedule. Often, I woke up in a hotel room wondering where I was, thinking about how I would function for the rest of the day. Some of the day's developments were not in my favor; the weather may have turned foul, my flight may have been delayed, my or my client's agenda may have changed. However, I do know that how I perceived the day was my choice. So, the moment I awoke, the first thing I said out loud was, **"This is going to be a great day."** This statement is an affirmation: it affirms and reinforces how I want to perceive the day. It also acts as a neutralizer to the often pessimistic and negative comments I am invariably exposed to each day.

Throughout the book I also discuss various affirmations and how you can develop them to support how you want to feel. If the average person would start each day with a personal affirmation, then reinforce that affirmation throughout the day, several positive developments would occur. There would be less of a chance of depression, feeling down or blue. There might be fewer arguments and breakdowns in business relationships, and certainly there would be less need for external stimulants—alcohol, coffee, sugar, Valium, marijuana, and other drugs—to create artificial feel-goods.

Using This Book to the Max

As you read this book and see a passage that interests you, copy that page or clip the appropriate passage and take action. Collect passages from every book you read, tape them to three-by-five cards and file them. Periodically, review the file to see if any passages apply at the moment. Alternately tape the card to your bathroom mirror, put a copy in your shaving or makeup kit for travel, and clip one to the sun visor in your car.

If you are a busy executive, have an assistant **preread** for you. An assistant, husband, wife, child, relative—almost anyone who can read—can become a prereader for you. Give your prereaders key words and themes that interest you. Then rely upon their judgment to highlight and underscore those articles and passages that you would choose. This doesn't stop you from reading other things that they may not have highlighted.

Read This Book with a Highlighter in Hand. When you finish a book no one else should want it. Mark up your books, fold the pages, and insert clips and notes throughout; use any tool that helps you get the most from this book. Many people prefer to keep their books in their original condition with dust covers intact. What is the purpose of most nonfiction books? Then use the book to extract information in an easily retrievable method.

Start Wherever You'd Like. Open to the index. Find information with which you identify, or begin with whatever interests you. Proceed backwards, then forwards if you like; you don't have to read the book sequentially. If your goal is to improve outcomes and have a great year every year, elect this method of reading nonfiction books.

Case Histories

Many case histories about real people and organizations are used throughout the book to illustrate and emphasize points. The majority of cases are based on my personal experiences with the organization or the person.

When possible, I identify the individual or corporation by name, with permission. In some cases, however, to avoid embarrassment or revealing confidential details, the names or other identification have been altered. All case histories are true and are used to support the EPOD Theory.

CHAPTER 1

Energy!

"All behavior is elected—we tend to repeat most often that behavior which is most affirmed (affirmed does not mean approved). The more frequently we repeat a behavior, the more comfortable we become with it."

—*Dave Yoho,* Managing Yourself & Others

A customer sees or hears your advertisement for something of which he may not have been aware. Your ads may explicitly or indirectly say:

"Come on in."
"Come see us."
"Call us."
"We want your business."
"We have what you want."
"We have a great price and great terms."
"This is a great place to do business."

Bolstered by stimulating messages, the customer visits your store, showroom, or model display in a high-energy state. He invests his time and effort to stop by or call you. Up to this point you've done everything right to capture the customer's attention.

Now the $64,000 question: Will the same level of energy, excitement, and enthusiasm that this potential customer felt when first learning about your product or service be maintained when he actually visits and/or interacts with you or your employees? The answer may depend on the environment you have created within your business.

Businesses make considerable efforts to improve product quality, ad copy, and even interior or exterior design. Yes, these things are important, but they don't address the fundamental reasons that customers keep coming back over the long term or decide not to do business at all. The high price of low energy may easily translate to low or no sales.

The Illusion of a High-Energy Environment

Let's look at a situation in which everything seems to be high energy, but in reality low energy is being transmitted to the customer.

You walk into a department store. You came because of an advertisement or a friend's recommendation. The showroom is dazzling. So far, this business lives up to your expectations and transmits the message that you made a good choice by coming in. At this moment, you have high energy.

Initially, no one greets you, but you figure that's okay. *Business is great,* you think, *and they probably have many things to take care of.* Finally, someone emerges and utters the classic archaic service question:

"May I help you?"

Despite the salesperson's intent, the overwhelming majority of people respond, "No thanks, just looking." The energy level drops and the impression of being in a special place dissipates. Why? As commonly spoken, the phrase "May I help you?" has been so overused that it is no longer perceived by the customer as a desire to help; it is received by many as an automatic, mundane, even trite greeting. It is unimaginative and certainly nonaffirming.

When I say to you, "May I help you?" the right side of your brain is not stimulated. You suspect that I am not really going to help you. I may contribute to a situation in which you will leave sooner than you would otherwise. The same phenomenon occurs if you call by phone and a voice answers, "XYZ Company, may I help you?"

How can customers be greeted so as to impart high energy? How do I get them to stay in my place of business or on the phone longer? Try offering an affirmation such as, "Thank you for coming in today," "We appreciate your coming in today," or "We are happy to have you here today." You don't often hear these kinds of greetings. When we offer these phrases the right side of the brain is stimulated and the listener is energized to feel better about the environment. Consequently, the chances are that they will stay longer.

> When you appeal to another person enthusiastically, romantically, musically, lyrically, or passionately, you stimulate the right side of the brain. Alternatively, the left side of the brain is stimulated by logic, reasoning, practicality, and data.

> When you call my company, we say, "Thank you for calling Dave Yoho Associates." The phrase "thank you" is an expression of gratitude; it stimulates feelings of well-being and helps develop harmonious relationships.

> Even if customers are skeptical about these different greetings, the power of the affirmations result in their overall feeling of well-being and increase the probability that they will want to stay or listen longer. Thus high energy transmitted receives a high-energy response.

Your business can transmit high energy too. Consider how customers feel when entering an EPOD-scripted store. They are enthusiastically welcomed with one of several responses:

> "Good morning. Thank you for shopping with us today!"
> "Thanks for visiting our store (or store name)!"
> "Hi. We're glad to see you! Thank you for shopping with us."
> "Good afternoon! We're glad you stopped in."

In all, an EPOD-trained host or hostess may offer the customer about a dozen different greetings, but a lame "May I help you?" is not one of them.

Customers are greeted within thirty seconds of entering a store, even if all sales staff are presently helping customers. In the latter case, a salesperson might excuse themselves momentarily by asking the customer whom they are currently serving, "I need your help," (pause) "Would you mind if I take a few moments to tell this person that someone will be with them shortly?" This question gains virtually a 100 percent affirmative response.

Temporarily freed, the salesperson uses one of the approved greetings with the new customer and then adds, "Thank you for your patience. Someone will be with you shortly." Both the initial customer and the one who just entered feel important and satisfied—all while maintaining a high energy level.

Does a High-Energy Approach Pay Off?

Examine how Wal-Mart, now the world's largest retailer, went from a small chain in rural markets to the dominant world leader in its field.

How did they compete with Sears, K-Mart, Montgomery Ward, J.C. Penney. and others? Certainly not with larger advertising budgets, classier locations, or interior design.

In their halcyon days they frequently attained greater sales per square foot, sales per outlet, and average purchase per customer visit than any of the larger, better-known, and established retailers. For the thirteen years ending in 1989, the Bentonville, Arkansas, discount chain raised its annual sales from $678 million to $16 billion.

A *New York Times* business journalist once described Wal-Mart as "the most dramatically successful retail company in the history of the U.S." A retail analyst for Smith, Barney, Harris, Upham and Company once predicted that "Wal-Mart would exceed the sales of Sears and K-Mart before it became a national chain." A retail analyst for Oppenheimer and Company said the company's growth rate was "one of the highest and its performance one of the most consistent in any economic environment." All of these pronouncements were correct, and the prediction came true.

The late Sam Walton, the company's founder, had been described as spreading equal parts of enthusiasm, evangelical spirit, and down-home glee to his employees (he called them associates), who in turn **transmitted this spirit and enthusiasm to customers.**

While this may sound oversimplified, consider that all major retailers buy in great quantities and can offer competitive low prices, so it was more than just a better price that created Wal-Mart's supremacy.

We believe an endemic factor was Wal-Mart's ability to constantly stimulate the customer into feelings of well-being, thus enticing the customer to stay in their store longer than in the stores of competitors: ergo, the longer they stayed in the store, the higher the average sale and the stronger the desire to return.

Sure it's more than just the greeting. It involved all in-store personnel and individual department personnel and managers stimulating the feelings of well-being and making you, the customer, feel you are in a place that cares about you.

Employees were called "associates" and were given incentives to produce. They were motivated to remain as part of the Wal-Mart family. As a result of this approach, each employee attempted to make Wal-Mart's customers feel the same.

The Wal-Mart story is an exciting case study in creating a high-energy environment directly related to what the customer was looking for.

Wal-Mart's techniques have since become the benchmark for mass merchandisers throughout the world. Now, what lessons can you learn from this case study about energy development for your business?

Beyond Customer Greetings

Effective customer greetings are important in transferring energy, but they are not the whole story. While customers are at your place of business, each time they call, and any other interactions they may have with you or your personnel represent **opportunities to convey high energy.**

Case #88: Nordstrom's with a Song

Walk into a Nordstrom's store and you might be struck by the excellent decor, the marble floors, the wide and inviting aisles, and the high-quality retail merchandise displays. But one of the things that originally set Nordstrom's apart from its competitors was the piano music provided for the customers.

Many customers did not realize at first that they were hearing live, not canned music. The original plan employed a formally clad piano player, and the customers' right brain loved it. Most stores had been designed with an atrium so that the music could be heard on every floor. The customers enjoyed the music, yet never consciously knew they were being stimulated. Add Nordstrom's policy of training salespeople to be upbeat and cheerful, and a high-energy environment was created in which customers were motivated to stay a little longer than average.

At Nordstrom's, while you were standing around waiting for your companion to try on a product, employees were trained to bring a chair for you and look after your packages. Nordstrom's employees were taught to extend to their customers the same hospitality they would receive when invited into someone's home. This atmosphere contributed to a feeling of well-being, and many customers stayed longer than planned. Longer stays frequently converted to larger sales.

A shopping environment can be perceived as an upbeat experience or a chore. Low-energy responses frequently convey to others that you do not care about them or see them as important. It may convey to customers that you don't attach significance to their presence. Often, customers themselves are not actively aware when they are in a low-energy environment. However, they do perceive that other business environments exist where they feel wanted, supported, and important. Shopping at Nordstrom's was not perceived as a chore but as a pleasant experience.

Ultimately customers tend to gravitate to companies with high-energy environments.

You May Have High Energy, but Are You Passing It On?

Many managers receive training in developing an effective staff. Some are proficient in personally maintaining high energy. Why, then, are they tolerant or ignorant of the low energy that some of their staff members transmit to customers?

I asked a client who owned several fast-food franchises, "How many people work for you?" His reply was, "About half of them." The eighteen-year-old part-time counter person may seem ideal to naturally exude high energy to customers. If so, it's a blessing for customer and company alike. However, it is impractical to assume that anyone, at any age, will automatically transmit high energy—the kind resulting in long-term customer patronization—without proper training and follow-up, and without a manager as an effective role model.

> In most environments when low-energy people are promoted to managerial positions, their low energy is perceived as "endorsed" by management; consequently, like a carrier of disease they pass it on.

Poorly trained counter persons transmit low energy all day and give hundreds of customers a poor impression of the company. Months pass and the counter person leaves. The manager barely remembers the individual because so many are hired in the course of a year. Yet, to customers who received the low-energy transmission, that now-departed counter person was their image of the business. When those same customers patronize a competitor and receive high-energy greetings and service, they will return, though not knowing precisely why.

The Most Important Things in Life Aren't Things

To transmit high energy to your staff, show them that you care about them by listening to them and greeting them with high energy. The energy is then transmitted to customers and passed on to others they encounter. High energy can be conveyed softly and quietly, without clamor. To transmit high energy, acknowledge each person as a unique individual with special wants and needs.

The level of energy you transmit to another is not dependent upon your age, sex, ethnic origin, education, or experience. It is based upon the way you feel about yourself, your business, and the people you serve. Put the following phrase at the top of your job description:

People are more important than products.

If you are interested in maintaining an atmosphere where motivation can occur, direct your energies toward your staff and they will take care of the product.

High Energy Is Elective

On any given day, at any given moment you can choose to transmit high energy. Here's an example of a sales rep heading to work. Guess how much energy he will be transmitting to customers:

On the way to work this morning he feels great. It's May, the birds are singing, his family is doing fine; it is going to be a good day. Yesterday he closed a big sale, and he is looking forward to a big commission check at the end of the week.

Then he gets stopped by a traffic cop and is handed a $50 ticket. Minutes later he gets a flat tire and is sidelined along the shoulder for thirty-five minutes.

When he does get to his office, his sales manager hands him a note that says yesterday's sale was cancelled because the customer's credit was not approved. The first prospect he sees is abrasive and condescending. The salesman feels he is verbally attacked several times in the span of about eight minutes. He is thankful when this interaction ends.

What amount of energy will he transmit for the rest of the day?

The answer is: The level he chooses or is assisted in developing by a high-energy manager. Of the next dozen people he sees he might sell three of them; he's done it before. Or, he could conclude that the whole day is shot and simply go through the motions of interacting with prospects.

The energy that he transmits to others will be a response to his internal decision-making process and/or how he is directed and stimulated in that environment. If he recognizes that a high energy level is in both his and the customer's best interests, the traffic ticket, the flat tire, the lost sale, and the abrasive prospect will all have little effect on how he interacts with the next prospect.

Your Life Energy Force: Maintaining a High Energy Level

You know when you are feeling up. It's unmistakable. External factors, however, can influence you. What you may not realize is that almost every element you are exposed to, such as foods, colors, other people, language, and news, can affect you positively or negatively, thus affecting your level of energy. However, you cannot proceed through your day waiting for or seeking positive stimulation in order to stay positive. In waiting, the positive influences may come too intermittently or not at all.

Many people use anticipation to stay positive, but this often boomerangs. Suppose you have been invited to what you know will be a fabulous party. You're up. You are really looking forward to this party. You are experiencing a simulated high. What happens once that party is over? You may equally experience a low. Unconsciously you may start to depend on outside stimulation or other forces to make you feel good.

Would you like to maintain a fairly even high on a consistent basis? It is possible to do this through positive thought, affirmations, and choice.

Case #17: Your Thoughts Influence Your Level of Energy

The marine colonel who stood in front of me was about six-foot-three and about 250 pounds. He looked like a weightlifter or a professional athlete. He was a volunteer from the audience I was addressing on research and findings in behavioral kinesiology (BK) and how this affects one's level of energy as measured with muscle testing.

I explained to the audience that as long as you're alive, you have a life energy force. It is affected by many things in your environment, such as food, clothing, art, poetry, music, and your feelings of well-being. Whether it's your decision to transmit high energy or not, certain factors add to your energy and others diminish it. For example, a negative thought or idea will at least temporarily diminish your energy, while a positive thought might do the opposite.

Now I was going to have to prove it, using the obviously skeptical colonel. I put him through a basic muscle test.

"Stick out your left arm at the shoulder," I said, facing him from about two feet away. He did. His arm looked like I could have swung from it. I explained the procedure. Then I told him that I could actually deplete his physical strength with a negative thought. This drew snickers from the audience and a smile from the colonel.

First, I gave him a positive message. Grasping his outstretched arm (as illustrated), I said, "Colonel, you seem like an officer we can be proud of. You are obviously a man of authority, a man with a commanding presence, a strong leader." I tried to push down on his arm but it would not budge.

He was pleased at my failed attempt to bring his arm down. Then with great seriousness I told him something that was completely untrue: I said, "But, there's a problem here. Did you know that scientific research has proven that, on the average, career military people are less intelligent than the general population?" Then I pushed down on his arm again, exerting the same pressure as before. His arm muscles weakened, and I was able to bring the colonel's arm down instantly. His jaw dropped just as fast, and the onlookers were dumbfounded. True or otherwise, negative statements create low energy.

Skeptics Become Believers. I have reenacted that demonstration hundreds of times in corporate boardrooms and in training seminars. The results are always the same. The skeptics remain skeptics until they go through the second half of the demonstration and I give them a negative suggestion.

The Ability to Choose

When I uttered false, negative statements to the colonel I temporarily weakened him. Through positive affirmations, silently reviewed, it would be possible for the colonel to resist my push, no matter what I said.

Psychiatrist Viktor Frankl, a World War II concentration camp survivor, observed that the people who survived the death camps were the ones who consciously and deliberately chose how they would think and act while inside the camp. Their basic thought process was that although their bodies were in captivity, their spirits were not. They could choose their own attitudes and remain free in the most fundamental sense of the term.

Dr. Frankl concluded that this ability to choose one's attitude enabled himself and others to survive, while others, many of whom were better treated and in better health, died.

Being Centered

When a subject is unaffected by the BK muscle test following a negative suggestion, it is called being "centered." The individual's energies are centered, and he or she is less vulnerable to stress. Remaining centered most of the time is an obtainable and appropriate goal for each of us.

Those who concentrate on their own self-worth instead of doubting themselves or wallowing in self-pity, who choose to see beauty instead of ugliness, who respond positively instead of negatively, are happier and more productive people, and maintain a consistent life energy force.

This is not an original insight. In many ways, what I have just written is almost a cliche of human behavior. Perhaps for that reason millions of people scoff at the idea that you can choose to have higher energy. Still, even among those who know the facts, many refuse to act on them.

Personal Energy Affects How We Live

In his book *Behavioral Kinesiology* (Harper & Row 1979), author Dr. John Diamond makes the observation that if you stand at a busy street corner in any city and watch people walk by, "most of these people seem like prisoners on the earth," rather than vibrant creatures, full of joy and glad to be alive.

The study indicated factors that lower body energy, including overly refined and unnatural foods, poor air quality, noise pollution and synthetic fabrics, as well as characteristics of the individual, including posture, the ability to handle stress, and negative thoughts or suggestions.

Factors that tend to increase body energy include positive thoughts, sound nutrition, fresh air, pleasant sounds and surroundings, natural fibers, and indeed, most things natural.

The Nutrition-Energy Link

The average American living to the age of seventy will consume approximately one hundred thousand pounds of food and twelve to fifteen pounds of medicine. Every time that food consumed contributes to a set of conditions which makes him ill, he seeks out a new medicine rather than deny himself the luxury of the offending food.

Most of the breads, meats, poultry, and other food items found in supermarkets today are laced with preservatives and other chemicals, largely for the benefit of the grower, processor, manufacturer, or seller. Seldom do any of these preservatives lead to a consumer benefit.

Medical science has made enormous health advances in the last several decades, including laser surgery, organ transplants, and miracle vaccines, yet these advances have been counterbalanced by the medical community's inability to convince the public that a poor or unbalanced diet is the principal cause of most illnesses and a major contributor to low energy.

Much of the medical profession still has on blinders to the many case histories that could provide an insight into the dietary changes most Americans need to enjoy good health. At his lectures, Dr. C. W. Cavanaugh used to say, "There is only one major disease, and that is malnutrition. All ailments and afflictions to which we may become heirs are directly traceable to this major disease."

Take a look at your business or personal environment. Identify the conditions that might lead to low energy and decide

- those that can be corrected immediately
- those that require short- or long-range strategies for correction

Case #49: From Low Morale to Higher Energy

Earl Windom, a senior vice president at a corporation with sales in excess of $1 billion, was experiencing a morale problem as an aftermath of his company's being acquired by a major public corporation. My company was brought in to analyze production, restaffing procedures, and sagging profits.

Low energy was a symptom of many conditions in the company's environment. By analyzing the following conditions and instituting rapid changes we initiated the processes that aided in a turnaround.

CONDITION: A confrontational attitude existed between the engineering and marketing departments which led to a slowdown in the work flow and constant bickering between department heads, who were supposed to be working cooperatively.

SOLUTION: A joint conference at which an experiment was proposed to eliminate the following three (3) conditions from phone language:

1) Remove value-judging words such as "should," "ought," and "must."
2) Remove adversarial language: more "we" and less "you vs. I."
3) Respond to all anger, hostility, and belligerence with an affirmation of understanding. (It's the situation—not the person)

AFTERMATH: The process took effect in approximately forty-five days. Within ninety days the measurable energy level had risen.

CONDITION: Managers working in windowless cubicles experienced low energy toward the end of eight- or ten-hour days.

SOLUTION: Change white fluorescent bulbs to full-spectrum bulbs, which imitate sunlight (contain reds and yellows) as do most incandescent bulbs.

AFTERMATH: Managers experienced increased energy functioning in the same offices.

CONDITION: Morning staff meetings offering coffee and doughnuts.

SOLUTION: Convinced management to serve natural fruit juices, fruit, and low-sodium, non-sugared breads and crackers.

AFTERMATH: A major transition problem here. The taste buds get used to elements (sugar, salt, caffeine) which reduce their energy. However, within three months, 40 percent of the participants had adopted most of the natural foods.

CONDITION: High level of negative language directed toward new parent company, flowing to line workers and low-entry positions, and ultimately to customers, vendors, and others.

SOLUTION: A series of seminars demonstrating through muscle testing how low energy is transmitted by negativity, convincing the participants that they were the first to suffer, not the other employees, customers, or vendors. Additionally, a contract was negotiated with all employees asking them to identify the language from which they would refrain for ninety days and to reconvene at that time for reevaluation and measuring.

AFTERMATH: Ninety-two percent of employees at this conference negotiated the contract. More than 60 percent stayed with the program for ninety days.

The positive as well as negative factors affecting individuals within any environment can be simply measured through the BK muscle test. Once these factors are identified and understood by those affected, effective solutions can be readily introduced.

Left- and Right-Brain Thinking

Left- and right-brain thinking influence the life energy force. Typically the left brain is the hemisphere that specializes in logical, analytical, and mathematical processing. It is where rational, factual thinking takes place. Other parts of the left brain specialize in linear, sequential, detailed modes of thinking that are used in planning, organizing, and administrative processing.

The right brain generally is the center of intuitive and insightful thinking where we can process information simultaneously and where conceptual thinking can take place. It is the location of our ability to synthesize as opposed to analyze. The right hemisphere also deals with specialized areas of interpersonal processing, emotional thinking, and music appreciation. It is where we recognize faces as contrasted to names and pictures versus plans; furthermore it is where we do our nonverbal thinking.

Frequently ideas, factual data, and statistics when presented in a high-energy mode get assessed rapidly in the left hemisphere and are then passed through to the right hemisphere where the decision-making process takes place. Conversely, many great ideas that would stimulate right-brain appraisal are presented in a low-energy manner and receive a low-energy response or none at all.

Characteristics of Left- and Right-Brain Thinking

Left: Tends to attract low-energy response	Right: Tends to attract high-energy response
Analytical and objective	Artistic and innovative, subjective
Regards time as continuous and sequential	Regards time as a series of discrete snapshots of past, present, and future
Recognizes conceptual similarities but not spatial ones	Recognizes spatial similarities but fewer conceptual ones
Verbal expression	Verbal and nonverbal expression, enthusiasm, gestures
Understanding through building basic concepts	Understanding through perception, image building
Limited intake of detail	Nearly unlimited intake of detail because of image-building capability

Achieving Hemispheric Balance. Reading the front page of your daily newspaper frequently lowers your energy because it mostly contains articles intended to alarm or spectacularize. The approach tends to be negative and judgmental, thus inducing low energy. Reading reports and technical data may have a similar effect. Conversely, reading positive messages, listening to upbeat music or humor, or viewing pictures and images that radiate positivity raise your energy level. People who take energy breaks during the day, who stop and recite an affirmation or the verse of a favorite poem, or look at a favorite picture or painting, greatly reduce their stress and help to move toward balance. Your immediate physical environment has a dramatic impact on your energy. Be selective of the circumstances in which you place yourself.

Love Yields High Energy

One of the most intriguing of Dr. John Diamond's findings for me was how the emotional state increases or decreases life energy. Diamond found that **feelings of love, faith, trust, encouragement, and gratitude were deep emotions that stimulated and in general strengthened individuals.** Conversely, feelings of hate, suspicion, fear, and resentment fostered weakness and imbalance.

You're In Charge

Dr. Bernie Siegel, an eminent physician and author, stated in his book *Love, Medicine, and Miracles*:

> Every tissue and organ in the body is controlled by a complex interaction among chemicals circulating in the bloodstream, the hormones secreted by our endocrine glands. This mixture is controlled by the "master gland," the pituitary gland located in the middle of the head just below the brain.

He also stated, "I am absolutely convinced that the feeling of support I grew up with gave me the belief that I could be what I wanted to be and guided me toward my desire to give and to heal."

When you give high energy you get high energy. When you pick up that phone and enthusiastically greet callers you get more enthusiastic responses. When giving your spouse or significant other a big hug you tend to get it back. The key is to stimulate your feelings of well-being before you address someone. At seminars I tell people who use the telephone, "Smile before you answer the phone or call someone."

You can control your energy level, health, environment, and destiny; the key ingredient is you.

Implementing a BK Regimen

Implementing a BK regimen in business is simple. Nevertheless, I find I have to proceed cautiously because the client and/or employee may perceive BK testing as a trick or gimmick. Yet, if I can convince them to observe the impact of high energy on themselves, peers, and customers, then they buy into the idea and slowly (but surely) high energy becomes a way of life.

Supporting a High-Energy Work Environment*
Replacement/Supplement Techniques

LOW ENERGY	HIGHER ENERGY	STRATEGY
Left-brain stimulation	Right-brain stimulation	Appeal to both, seek balance
Logic, practicality, technical data	Enthusiasm, emotion	High-energy environment
Value judging (should, ought, must)	Nonjudgmental language	Behavior modification
Criticism	Acknowledgment, assessment, observation data	Change methods of review
Hard rock music (most)	Classical, modern jazz, some country/western	Background music in your home or place of business
Smoking (presence of)	Nonsmoking environment	Restricted areas, policy

---

*Power Linguistics™—The science and practice of powerful communication, Dave Yoho Associates (a seventeen-year study)

LOW ENERGY	HIGHER ENERGY	STRATEGY
Fast food	Fruits, nuts, grains, low-sodium crackers, whole grain bread	Coffee break, lunch breaks, and conferences
Sugar	Honey	Dispensary in commissary, kitchenettes

Determining Your Own Energy Level

The following quiz will help you gauge how you currently apply ENERGY:

Points:	[0]	[1]	[2]	[3]
	Never	Occasionally	Frequently	Always

1. Do I attempt to activate my energy system or do I wait for others or other circumstances to bring me a 'feel good'?
2. Do I transmit enthusiasm in my voice when I greet others and answer the phone?
3. Do I reflect high energy in my eye to eye contact and handshake?
4. Do I use gestures and body movements when I am explaining or attempting to convince others?
5. Do I hum, sing or recite in my shower and when alone in my car?
6. Do I exhibit undivided interest in the conversation of others?
7. Do I maintain a balance—neither a comedian nor a grouch—friendly, yet not overly intimate?
8. Do I not permit setbacks or disappointments to reduce my energy on a daily basis?
9. Do I avoid negative thoughts early in the day which influences my production and interpersonal relationships later?
10. Do I smile and laugh spontaneously?

If you scored under 25, the energy that you transmit is not sufficient to ensure that your staff, customers and business environment reverberates with an energy level sufficient for success. Your goal is to consistently score 25 or higher.

The best way to increase your score is to copy the questions for which your score is low and prominently post them on your bathroom mirror, near your desk, or wherever convenient. For the next twenty-one days, simply read them each morning. Then take the test again; your new score may surprise you.

EPOD Tactics

- Don't depend on others for your feel-goods. Manufacture them each day through personal affirmations and self-talk.
- Change the way you answer your phone and be cautious how long you allow a caller to be on hold. Thirty seconds on hold can seem like an eternity.
- To transmit a high level of energy to others, give them your undivided attention. Listen to them intently as if nothing else exists. Respond with an affirmation, such as, "Thank you for bringing that to my (our) attention. We sure do appreciate your business/the opportunity/your continued support. . . ."
- Whenever possible, put yourself in the company of positive, high-energy people.
- The traditional corporation operates on left-brain thinking, utilizing logic, empirical data, statistics, systematized procedures, and a structured organizational chart, while a traditional entrepreneur often concentrates on right-brain direction, including large doses of creativity, rapid changes, rugged individualism, being reactive, and rejecting old ways and methods. Attempt to blend the two concepts. When there is a balance of right- and left-brain thinking and a permission for each to exist at every level of the business, a dynamic organization emerges.
- You do not need to rely on someone else's opinion as to how something will affect you. You can become your own energy advisor.
- Follow the BK dictum: "Choose those things for which you test strong; avoid those things with which you test weak."
- Take frequent energy breaks, reciting your affirmation, particularly at the start of each day and during any stressful situation.
- Listen to revitalizing music or positive attitude tapes.
- Concentrate on pleasant thoughts and positive images of yourself and others.

- Hug your spouse, children, companions.
- Practice smiling.
- Think, walk, and act with high energy.
- Dwell on positive thoughts such as love, faith, trust, gratitude, and courage.
- Practice high-energy techniques daily to continually raise your life's energy and positively affect those around you.
- Enthusiasm is a key ingredient of high energy and it is contagious; find out why. Look up the definition of enthusiasm (*entheos*/Gr.). You will be surprised.

CHAPTER 2
Persuasion: A Vital Element to Your Success

"The measure of all communication is the outcome. If you are not getting the outcomes you want, change your pattern of communication."
—*Dave Yoho,* Power Linguistics™

No element of the EPOD Theory evokes more misunderstanding than **Persuasion**. It is the hidden or elusive skill, and those in leadership positions cannot succeed without it. Ministers, lawyers, and guidance counselors become peak performers only when they understand it. Salespeople cannot maintain a career or present their wares efficiently if they don't master the skill.

The art and science of persuasion is frequently misinterpreted, highly undervalued, and in most organizations poorly taught.

If the term "highly persuasive" conjures up images for you of spellbinding speeches, manipulation, or high-pressure selling, you are misinformed. The skill of persuasion is derived from a science governed by basic psychological laws.

During seventeen years of research to produce a body of work entitled **Power Linguistics**™—The Science and Practice of Powerful Communication, we uncovered people who used

Power Linguistics is the trademarked property of Dave Yoho Associates.

persuasion in a powerful, positive way. Many of these people, however, were not able to measure or even understand their skill level, and only a small percentage could pass their level of information on or train others.

In numerous Fortune 500 companies where we interacted with management and line people, we met seemingly charismatic personalities whose major skill in outperforming their contemporaries was directly related to their ability to influence and persuade those whom they managed in such a manner as to exceed goals and outperform other similar groups. We discovered that they frequently appealed to very basic human drives and needs found in those people and applied their persuasive skills in such an easily understood manner as to get immediate results.

We had the opportunity to work with executives whose key responsibility was to turn around organizations suffering from weak sales and low profitability, and even those in bankruptcy. In such cases, the environment of the culture was often low energy and exhibited many layers of pervasive negativity. Many of these turnaround specialists developed immediate believability. They were frequently perceived as experts even though they may have had little experience in the business or industry in which they were currently interacting.

Dr. Robert Cialdini, author of *Influence—Science and Practice* (Allyn and Bacon, 2001), has written the most compelling treatise that we examined in terms of persuasion. Among his many conclusions, he states:

> Amid the teaming complexity of life, a well-selected expert seems to offer value and efficient shortcuts to good decisions.

Within this brief statement, Cialdini touches on the concept of perception being reality. People perceive they have an expert leader, and the majority are willing to follow the advice and direction proffered.

Cialdini further explains that persuasion is governed by basic principles that can be taught, learned, and applied. He says, "By mastering these principles, executives, managers and salespeople can bring scientific rigor to the business of securing consensus, winning concessions and making deals." He is quick to explain, however, that for long-range effect, the rules of ethics apply to the science of social influence. Not only is it ethically wrong to trick or trap others into ascent; it is ill advised in practical terms. Dishonest or high-pressure tactics work only in the short run, if at all. Their long-term effects are malignant.

In later chapters, we discuss case histories of some of the more influential persuaders we have met and how this less-understood skill of persuasion, when used effectively, pays big dividends.

Removing the Blocks to More Persuasive Language

To persuade someone to do something requires finding out the true basis of their mind-set and value system, then showing them a way to get what they want through your medium. This is true whether you are selling products or ideas. If I can learn enough about you, your values, and what your needs are, then I can show you ways to get what you want.

Your language and the way you use it usually determines your ability to persuade. Through Power Linguistics we found that many words and phrases, because of misuse and overuse, are not persuasive; instead they tend to neutralize otherwise effective communication and social interaction. Overused words, such as personal pronouns (I, me, my) and meaningless adjectives (fantastic, fabulous), are often neutralizers or turnoffs.

Phrases that halfheartedly ask about one's health, "How are you feeling?" or phrases that direct an individual, "You really should try this," have about the same effect as the archaic retailers' greeting, "May I help you?" These phrases transmit low energy to others; hence they attract low energy. Here's a brief list of de-persuasive language, from my Power Linguistics research and program:

Fabulous   To tell the truth
Brand-new   Do you follow me?
Unbelievable   You know . . .
                          May I help you?

I, we, me
Out of this world
Like . . . like . . . like
Between you and me

How are you today?

What's up?
You should, ought, or must

Measure how frequently these and similar words and phrases are used by those attempting to get positive outcomes from their communications. Overused cliches have the same effect.

In contrast, our research indicates the following words and phrases have power; they affirm or acknowledge others. They aid in the development of rapid rapport. Most readers are familiar with all of these, yet they use them too infrequently in their attempts to communicate:

Unexcelled	Protection	Dependable	You, your
Assurance	Experience	Pride	Share
Why is that?	Genuine	Tell me more	Help
Enjoyment	Expert	Security	Dedicated
Quality	Popular	Convenience	Save
Prestige	Confidence	Peace of mind	Invaluable
Service	Efficient	Original	Love
Courtesy	Durable	Fun	Positive results
Growth	Reputation	Stimulating	Easy
Relief	Necessary	Modern	Proven
Stylish	Successful	Health	Guarantee
Rewarding	I appreciate	I understand	Discovery

Thank you for (preceding request)   And your preference is . . .

Some of these words and phrases reflect feelings, while others offer believable promises of safety, security, fun, happiness, and solutions to problems.

> To effectively use more powerful and persuasive words and to measure their effects, select and circle three (3) words from above. Use them in your language for the next 21 days, then select three more and repeat the process.

In these examples, **Persuasion** is how you use language to ensure that someone's experience is pleasant and comfortable enough that they will be willing to accept what you would like them to do or try. Energy and persuasion are closely linked; in combination they become formidable. Without the appropriate energy, it is difficult to be as persuasive as you might wish.

Hedging Language Does Little to Persuade

Between neutral language and persuasive words and phrases comes hedging. Hedging phrases are those that mean little or nothing, or those that disguise what one really thinks or feels. Examples include, "You know best," "Is that so?" or "You might not believe this."

One of my favorite anecdotes provides an excellent illustration of hedging language that fails to persuade. It's about an Irish priest during Holy Week, who has a heavy bias against the British.

> On Friday, the priest gives his best sermon. He says to the congregation:
> "This is the night that we celebrate the Last Supper. 'Twas at the Last Supper that Jesus spoke to the Apostles and said, 'One of you will betray me.'
> "And he looked at Peter and said, 'Will it be you?' And Peter said, 'No, it will not be me, Master.'
> He looked at James and said, 'James, will it be you?' And James said, 'No, it will not be me, Savior.'
> Then he looked a Judas and said, 'Judas, will it be you?' And Judas said, 'Look 'ere, Guv'nor. . . .'"

Language That Is Not Persuasive

Being persuasive does not mean talking down to others, downgrading your competitors' ideas or products, ridiculing alternative approaches, or resorting to negative language. Persuasive language is a science of word usage that eliminates the need for deception, high-pressure negativity, gossip, or put-downs.

Unfortunately, our political system may be devolving to the point where candidates are elected based on how effectively they are able to portray other candidates as inept, unworthy, or dishonest rather than addressing how they as a candidate will handle the critical issues of the day.

Attempts to be persuasive using negative language are detrimental to both the speaker and the listener.

Case #40: Business Meets the Press

Curt Jones, age thirty-eight, is newly assigned as general manager of a medium-sized division of a major corporation. His record of success is impressive, and he has a reputation for being tough, hardworking, and hard-nosed. He has brought several members of his team with him from another division.

He received his new post because this division has been plagued by morale and production problems. It also has been drowning in red ink for two years. Curt's team focuses immediately on the problems. First, the assessment group evaluates personnel; then the components of the business such as production, purchasing, marketing, sales, and finance are examined.

Next, Curt and his staff develop both long- and short-range plans. They restructure the marketing plan, the operating system, and the organizational chart. Then they prepare a list of personnel changes, including managerial ones. Finally, they devise an orderly transition plan. All this is accomplished within seventy-five days.

Curt schedules a press conference to help ensure continuing industry and market base support, as well as to condition the local community to the changes.

During the press conference Curt is responsive to the questions regarding his background and the goals for this division. Several members of the press start to use zinger-type questions and negative reflections, but Curt is no stranger to this kind of interaction:

Press: Mr. Jones, we understand that your transition plan calls for furloughing seventy-five to one hundred plant and middle-management persons, is that correct?

Curt: That is correct.

[Bravo, Curt. No speeches—just facts.]

Press: Have you considered the economic effect this will have on these people and this community?

Curt: Yes we have, and we regret the need to make this kind of decision, but it's either that or shut down the plant and get out of this business.

[Here, Curt's tough management is showing through. However, it invites the press to pose the next question.]

Press: Do I understand that closing the plant and discontinuing the business were options?

Curt: Obviously if a company is not making money with a product line, they would be wise to get out of the business quickly. We chose other alternatives.

[Tough again, Curt. The general statement about companies getting out of the business if they can't make a profit is good business logic. Hmm, I wonder if the press heard it that way?]

Press: Based on your background and success in the company's other divisions, I'm sure they have confidence in your plan. But, suppose it doesn't work, or doesn't work as rapidly as anticipated? Could we expect to see more layoffs or even more drastic measures, such as the other option you mentioned?

Curt: Anything is possible; however, I'm reasonably certain that our proposed changes will be effective. It is our intent to keep a check on all facets of the business and the changes we have directed. We'll know soon if we are doing enough things right. I have asked my staff to evaluate our overall progress in 120 days.

[Curt, you are an action guy, it's obvious, and you are sending out a message: give us results or more changes will follow.]

The press conference continues with this type of interaction. The reporters leave with a clear picture of Curt's tough style, assured that he is the kind of manager who can pull this company out of its financial morass, bring the plant back to the full operations it once enjoyed, and reinstate the positive economic impact on the community.

The next day, the business section of the largest local newspaper devotes the front page to Curt's press conference. It praises his tough style and his long-range plans. Consider, however, some of the highlighted statements:

- New general manager says, "We'll make a profit or shut down."
- "We will lay off seventy-five to one hundred people. It's purely a business decision."
- New general manager says he will reevaluate in four months. [Hold your breath] More layoffs could follow.
- New GM says, "I want results in 120 days or else."

Now evaluate the impact of the statements above, even though they have been printed out of context. Worker morale is affected: we all tend to react to what is in a newspaper, seldom assessing validity. Those who face an impending layoff, await further cuts, and aren't sure of where they stand are all affected by the newspaper's portrayal of tough management.

Those who may have a relatively secure position with seniority or other special status detect in Curt's tough management stance the message: "Either we make the necessary changes quickly to achieve profits, or we close down this company."

The product that this company manufactures is in a highly competitive field. Each employee's productivity is vital to keeping the company competitive. Stability, product availability, turnaround time, and follow-through service are major factors that affect market share.

Within two days of the article, the competitors' salespeople are armed with copies of it. With subtle references, innuendo, and mild distortions, they paint a vivid picture throughout the sales territories of the extremely tentative and shaky position of Curt's division.

The Preparation to Be Persuasive

Curt failed to use persuasive language, and as a result he had a less than desired outcome, to the detriment of the company and himself. To prepare himself for such an event, he could have shared his presentation in advance with his key staff members to better gauge the potential impact of his language. Curt could even have held a mock press conference to bring to the surface any issues that might be contentious. Also, he could have circulated a carefully worded statement, recognizing that the press often uses segments of prepared messages and transcripts.

To preempt some of the zinger-type questions, Curt could have developed and circulated a list of ten to twelve likely questions along with answers.

Because Curt did not undertake these exercises (a **Discipline**—more in a later chapter) the language that he used, and hence his attempt to be persuasive was ineffective. It would be hard to assess Curt as a poor general manager, yet by using non-persuasive language he's made a tough situation even tougher.

The Potential in Every Encounter

Persuasive language is an effective tool to impress a new or first-time customer, but it is much more. It is a manner of speaking that uses language and responses to convey the message: "We are in business to serve you." Many companies want to provide effective customer service, yet the one-on-one capability to offer persuasive language that satisfies the **customer's perception of service** is often lacking in business.

Each time the phone rings or a new customer comes to your company, the potential exists for a sale and/or a long-term relationship. Each customer with a service request (or complaint) represents another opportunity for your business.

How Do You Say "Hello"? Companies that recognize the importance of using appropriate language actually script customer greetings and ensure that all employees use them. As Curt's experience illustrates, the use of persuasive language is too important to be left to chance.

At Dave Yoho Associates, how we greet customers and callers is so vital to our persuasiveness, and hence the environment we choose to maintain, that **we follow a script**, which starts with the affirmation: "Thank you for calling Dave Yoho Associates." People tell me, "Wow, that person who answers the phone for you sure does a good job." Other people tell me, "You've had the same receptionist for about five years, right?" Callers don't realize it is not always the same receptionist; it is consistent, persuasive language that is utilized by whoever answers the phone.

Believable Promise. Persuasive language offers a believable promise, much like effective copy in a printed advertisement. Persuasive language means addressing the customer or prospect at his or her level of reception, which is not easy to do given that our society is egocentric. We think that sharing our experience of the world or of a product can persuade others. Our society and much training teaches first-person language as both introductory and dominant within efforts to communicate. This is particularly true in sales training:

> "I believe . . . ," "I think . . . ," "I did this . . . ," "I did that . . ."
> "I want to show you . . . ," "I want to tell you . . ."
> "Our company . . . ," "Our group . . . ," "My product . . ."
> "Our method . . . ," "Our solution . . . ," "My opinion is . . ."

The people to whom you speak listen in second person. References to their values, wants, needs, and feelings are most effective. This style of speaking often requires a suppression of first-person references. The solution is to become more other-centric and to put more "you" and "your" into the language (particularly at the start of your discussion) and less "I," "we," and "our."

> The first rule of an effective sales presentation (oral or printed) is to start with the words "you," "your problem," "your needs," etc.

What the Customer Needs, Not What You Have

When someone asks for information on a computer, copier, or almost any product, and you immediately reply, "We have all kinds here, so I think we can take care of you," you are *not* using persuasive language. Why?

> Because your focus is on what you have and not on what the prospect wants or needs.

When you address me as a customer or prospect, your goal is to find out what I need so that you can be persuasive. First, determine the key features I seek. After listening to me, and asking response-type open-ended questions, you find out about my needs. Cataloguing what I say, you are in a far better position to offer a solution to my needs. Now you can offer what you have. If you've done your job correctly, I will be more receptive to what you recommend, even though the solution to my needs may be the item you had in mind all along.

> **Credentials Not Required.** Persuasion has little to do with credentials in its early stages. The salesperson who talks about his/her latest success, education, background, experience, company supremacy, or the like is not employing persuasion. Persuasiveness is predicated on how receptive you are to others and what's on their mind. Remember the old bromide: "People don't care how much you know, until they know how much you care."

Increase your persuasiveness in general by **learning as much as possible about your customers' values and interests**. To be persuasive, transmit the feeling within your message and do it with second-person rather than first-person language:

Persuasive Intent	*Persuasive Language*
"I (we) care about you, your interests."	"What prompted your call/visit to us?"
"I (we) care about your values and opinions."	"What would you like to accomplish/avoid?"
"I (we) want to understand you, and what you'd like to achieve."	"What have you tried in the past?" "How do you want this to look?" "What outcome do you desire?"

You then draft and deliver a message that fits their needs, without resorting to egocentric language. If you can do so honestly, convey that you or others you know have faced some of the same problems as the customer. You want to convey the message, "I come from the same place, and together we can solve your particular problem."

The next time you go to buy carpet, observe whether the salesperson asks:

- "How many people are in your home?"
- "How many children do you have?"
- "What functions take place in this room?"
- "What is the room size?"
- "How long have you lived in this house?"
- "What kind of floor covering do you have now?"

This is persuasive language. The salesperson does the asking, the customer does the responding. The proper use of these questions indicates that the salesperson cares not just about making a sale, but about providing a product or service that meets your needs and specifications.

Persuasion Is the Key to Effective Customer Service Departments

Effective, persuasive language is particularly important in the customer service (or complaint) department of companies of all sizes. In successful companies the customer relations staff is taught that its members are just as important to a company's persuasiveness in developing long-term customers as the front-line sales staff are. They are also taught:

Problems created their jobs.
The customer is a necessary asset to a business.
Calming an excited, demanding or upset customer is a challenge, not a confrontation.

The person with the greatest skill level is the one who usually ends up being in charge.

> The issue is not who is right or who is wrong—the real issue is customer satisfaction. Effective customer relations reps learn that while customers may or may not be right, their feelings and perceptions are always important, and the effective service is based solely on customer perception. Thus the statement, "The customer is always right," is a perception.
> —*Dave Yoho,* Customer Satisfaction Selling

Companies who train their service departments to respond to customers by expressing the message, "Thank you for calling this to our attention," or "Please give me all the facts, and do you mind from time to time if I ask questions?" fare better in the long run, incur less customer dissatisfaction, and retain service representatives who feel good about their roles.

Case # 56—No Malice from Alice

Alice Martin, a customer service representative in the auto parts department of a large, metropolitan store, is skilled in using effective, persuasive language.

She receives a phone call from an irate customer who is seeking to exchange an expensive set of custom wheels; he's been back to the store twice already, and the latest set contains blemishes. While the customer is shouting and using heated language, Alice gets the necessary information to solve the problem. The customer, growing more impatient, eventually explodes.

"Lady," he screams, "you can take these wheels and shove 'em up your. . . ." The remarks were uncalled for and in bad taste, but Alice keeps her cool.

Calmly she replies, "Sir, I appreciate your offer, but I'm already dealing with a radio and set of hubcaps that were directed to the same part of my anatomy yesterday." Then she pauses.

The customer cannot believe his ears. He pauses, asks her name, and within forty minutes is standing at her counter laughing. The wheels are exchanged and his problem is solved. Alice retains a customer for her company—perhaps for *years*—because of her persuasive, effective language skills.

If your score is 15 or less, you require a serious revision of your interactive language.

If your score is 18 or more, concentrate more on using power words and phrases.

If your score is 23 or more, you are on the right track.

With a score of 25 or more, simply keep doing what you are doing; you are being persuasive.

Remember, in areas where your score is low, simply posting the question over your desk and reading it for a minimum of twenty-one days will help you to improve your ability in that area. You will be conscious of your desire to improve.

Points:	[0]	[1]	[2]	[3]
	Never	Occasionally	Frequently	Always

1. Do I refrain from using first person language (I, we, me) and instead use second person language (you, your, yours) in conversations with others?
2. Do I avoid stereotypical, low persuasive greetings, i.e., "May I help you?" in place of more positive language?
3. Do I avoid cliche phrases such as: unbelievable—awesome—out of this world—between you and me—this is the truth—do you follow me?
4. Do I avoid value judging words and phrases such as: you should—you ought to—you must?
5. Do I avoid using phrases which have become meaningless such as: "How are you today"—"How are you feeling"—"How is the weather"?
6. Do I avoid trying to win arguments at the risk of breaking down relationships?
7. Do I listen fully before I respond?
8. Do I avoid 'talking too much' to convince others what I 'know'?
9. Am I patient with the responses of others?
10. Do I avoid 'overtalk' with those that seem more affable and attentive?

EPOD Tactics

- A powerful key in the use of persuasive language is talk less, acknowledge more, and listen longer.
- Use affirming language on a regular basis.
- Include power words and phrases in your daily conversation.
- Ask questions. When in doubt, ask another question.
- Every time you revisit a prospect or one comes into your place of business, include an appreciation phrase very early in the conversation:

I appreciate your time today.
I appreciate your continuing business.
I appreciate your seeing me today.
I appreciate the order recently received.
I appreciate your calling [xyz] to my attention.

- To be exceptionally persuasive means to convert confrontational situations into successful relationships.
- Pause four seconds before you respond to a complaint or an objection, and almost always respond with a question. It shows you care about what was said. It sets the tone for a response, and the response broadens your ability to understand the circumstances.
- Practice your upbeat, persuasive techniques in front of a mirror, on the phone, and with your family. In the last case, you will receive immediate payback.
- Always start your memos and letters with a second person reference instead of a first-person reference ("you," "your" vs. "I," "we," "me"). It's called "writing for the reader" and has automatic (yet nonconscious) appeal to the recipient.
- Eighty percent of your customers will respond to effective customer service. About 20 percent of your customer base (we'll call them the "A"s) will continue to do business with you despite numerous inequities in your customer service.
  Another 20 percent, the "B"s, will not be satisfied no matter what you do if there is a minor breakdown or

glitch. The remaining 60 percent of your customer base, the "C"s, can be influenced with better-than-average customer service techniques.

The "A"s and "C"s compose 80 percent of your customer base and represent a strong reason to continually develop a customer service program.

CHAPTER 3
Optimism

The mind does not know the difference between the real or the imagined, so optimism is a choice.

Optimism is an outlook that the brain generates. The mind does not know the difference between what is real and imagined. You bring optimism into your environment much like you bring energy: by **choosing it**. As optimism usually begets a positive response from others, pessimism usually gets a negative response. Years of research indicate that five to ten minutes of sustained negativity can affect the central nervous system for up to twenty hours or more.

We live in a world where the presence of negativity seems to escalate daily. The level of pessimism generated from the media's reporting style affects the way we look at education, matrimony, and business decisions, and even the way the stock market responds.

Frequently, a major corporation is profitable but slightly below forecast. Within twenty-four hours of the news report, a stock's value declines. People read about the increase of a specific disease and begin to ponder whether certain minor irregularities or symptoms they have experienced is truly the dreaded disease. Although we are an affluent society with much to be thankful for—including an economy far superior operatively than any other in the world, and with all the advances of science including medicine here to serve our purpose—the levels of depression in American society are increasing daily. The prevailing wisdom says that often high levels of pessimism are the precursor to states of depression.

Dr. Martin Seligman, a noted researcher and author of *Learned Optimism* (Knopf, 1990), makes this point at the risk of oversimplifying the issue. Those who operate at a level of high optimism believe that defeat or a setback is not their fault. They see it as a product of circumstances, bad luck, or conditions brought on by others. Conversely, pessimists in the same circumstances tend to see the defeat as being the outgrowth of ineptitude, poor decision making, and failure to exercise wise judgment.

In his research, Dr. Seligman came to the conclusion that many pessimists see their attitude and reaction to circumstances as being so deeply rooted as to be permanent. Seligman balances this statement and in reliance on his research says, "I have found that pessimism is escapable. Pessimists can learn to be optimists." He points out, though, that optimism is more complicated than whistling a happy tune on a dreary day or mouthing platitudes such as "Every day in every way I am getting better and better." The conclusions reached by the studies of Seligman and other leading psychologists and psychiatrists in the field of optimism indicate that it requires learning a new set of cognitive skills.

Optimism is the ability to recognize that **opportunities that await you may have no connection to anything that came before**. Optimism is a deep-down, chosen feeling that you can accomplish your goals.

The way the average individual tends to view life and the control he/she has over it determines the level of skills they possess in working towards optimism. Many individuals come to this process naturally.

> The pessimist says, "When I die." The optimist says, "If I die."
>
> The pessimist says, "Here are the statistics that govern." The optimist says, "Those statistics don't include me."
>
> The pessimist says, "Because I am smaller, they can defeat me." The optimist says, "I am faster than those clumsy oafs, they'll never catch me."
>
> The pessimist says, "The smartest man in this industry said this can't be done." The optimist says, "I never said that."

When we overestimate our inabilities, lack of skills, or knowledge, outside forces take control and shape our future. Again, referring to Dr. Seligman's research, if you perpetually believe that misfortune is your fault, this belief can become enduring and undermine most things you attempt to do, thus creating for the pessimist a reinforcement of his/her own ineptitude.

It is important to extend a caution that merely daydreaming, having fantasies, or idealizing certain situations does not necessarily aid performance. However, high-level optimists believe that failure or defeat is essentially a temporary setback; the bad outcome had specific causes, and now they have enhanced experience and information to incorporate as they reapproach the task. Essentially, defeats and failures are part of the learning process for optimists' future success.

In the best-selling book *The Road Less Traveled*, author Dr. M. Scott Peck opens the book with the statement, "Life is difficult." As individuals and society become more affluent, the level of complexity increases. How then do we deal with the escalating need to solve problems, change direction, increase our skills, and combat the ever-growing use of negativity to gain attention?

Optimism Is Optional

In most situations, you can opt to choose between optimism or pessimism. For example, suppose sales haven't been up to par in the last year so the sales manager assembles her staff for a closed-door meeting. She begins by saying, "We have got to improve sales. Otherwise, we may not be in business by next year."

Or, suppose the same manager chooses to say, "We have a high potential to do a lot more business. While we are not meeting our goals now, our research indicates that we can, with some adjustments. We can do better because we are better." Which statement is likely to generate optimism and positive action on the part of the staff?

Following poor first-quarter sales, the wise manager takes an optimistic view about what can be done during the year's remaining three quarters. The pessimistic manager, consciously and subconsciously, prepares for a disastrous year. Feelings are disseminated in one way or another to the employees and the customers. Sure enough, the company has a bad year (self-fulfilling prophecy).

Imagine being in real estate sales and thinking to yourself, *Unemployment is up and the mortgage market is down. It may be the wrong time to be in this business. How did I get myself into this situation?*

Now, contrast these thoughts with the following: *Home ownership is the best way to invest money for most middle- and lower-income people. This is the time for me to be in the real estate business, because weaker Realtors aren't going to cut it. Most sales will go to the best-informed, hardest-working agents like myself.*

Another example: You sell cars for a living and your perception tells you that everyone is buying the competitor's car. You start thinking, *Theirs is a great car, but . . . who wants to drive down the pike in the same car as everyone else? We have a great opportunity to sell our cars now.*

Examine how the process of pessimism can influence attitudes where all participants consider they have an option. As you examine these examples, imagine that the pessimist becomes reinforced by poor, weak outcomes, frequently leading to a higher level of pessimism and melancholia, which in turn create a level of depression. Nothing herein diminishes the concern for those who suffer depression. However, as early as the mid-1960s, researchers Joseph Wolpe and Tim Beck drew the conclusion that mild depression is frequently a symptom caused by repetitious negative thoughts.

A negative viewpoint could have been selected: *Theirs is the hottest selling car on the market. Yup, everyone's buying it. We can't compete with that car; half the people that come into our showroom ask me how our cars measure up to that one. I might as well fold up the tent; there's no use even trying to compete with it.*

Gifted people—those with innate skills in art, music, or theater—have failed to achieve their potential because of their lack of self-confidence imposed by their pessimistic attitude.

Again, quoting Dr. Seligman: "A composer may have all the talent of Mozart or even passionate desire to succeed. However, if he does not possess optimism, ultimately he will not produce the music which he is capable of composing. He will not try hard enough."

It is not uncommon to believe your current challenges are greater than most of your contemporaries. Examine the following case study.

Case #18: The Chrysler Turnaround— Optimism Is Optional

During the 1980s, Chrysler Corporation found itself in a difficult situation. They were the smallest of the "Big Three" (G.M., Ford, and Chrysler). Together this group dominated the U.S. auto market.

Chrysler had the smallest piece of the market, and they had a history of producing well-engineered cars in a range of price models—although their designs seemed to be the least appealing to U.S. auto buyers.

Now put into the mix a management style at Chrysler that had accumulated billions in losses and an almost equal amount not available for their unfunded pension/retirement plan.

Would you be anxious to take on the turnaround management job? One man was: Lee Iacocca. He paid his former employer, Ford Motors, $1 million to buy out his non-compete contract, thus enabling him to become chairman and CEO at Chrysler for $1 per year, plus stock options and an incentive based on Chrysler's return to profitability. Doesn't sound like good arithmetic, does it?

Optimism in business involves decoding a set of facts and feeding it to others in a manner that prompts positive action. Persuasiveness and optimism thus are inextricably linked, as are energy and optimism.

Consider the optimism of Lee Iacocca at the height of Chrysler's difficulties. He was faced with many complex problems, among them financial insolvency, poor profitability, weak and ever-shrinking sales, and low morale.

Anyone who is familiar with Lee Iacocca's management style could not assess it as being soft. Given the circumstances he was facing, equivalent to reviving a bankrupt company, no one but a tough, optimistic manager would take the job.

As one of the Chrysler executives later related to me, from the beginning Iacocca maintained an optimistic tone in crucial policy changes with the Chrysler dealers. Iacocca first stressed the dealers' importance to the corporation and explained how decision-changing policies would affect them. He emphasized their prominence in the corporate marketing structure. Then, to engender the dealers' support he imparted a message something like this:

> I know this is how we used to do it. However, we simply cannot continue the practice [Chrysler's maintenance of a large automobile inventory to meet dealers' future needs, a costly and impractical system].
>
> I need your cooperation in reducing this current inventory and in the transition to the "you order it, we make it" philosophy. I know with your help we can make this the strong company it once was.

Iacocca's is an example of a strong manager soliciting internal help to implement a tough plan by using appropriate, persuasive, optimistic language. This style also reveals how Iacocca convinced more than 450 top managers to leave the relative security of financially sound companies to join a debt-ridden company whose position was derided by the competition, Congress, the press, and the stock market.

He did not accomplish the turnaround by saying, "We'll either turn this company around in a year or two or close it." Yet many managers and business owners use negative, fear-motivated pessimism daily in an effort to implement their plans. Then they deride participants for having low morale.

Iacocca was criticized and denigrated by the press, many lawmakers, and an astute corps of economists who predicted Chrysler's demise. His optimism within the Chrysler Corporation, however, was translated as, "Together we can do this. With your cooperation we can make this work. We'll build this into a successful, profitable company again with your help."

As the turnaround proceeded, Iacocca was roundly criticized for mentioning Chrysler's positive cash position. The financial press called it braggadocio. One well-known newscaster labeled it an ego-centered statement. Nevertheless, consider the impact this statement had on dealers, suppliers, employees, and consumers. It was the same as saying, "With your help we've turned this company around and soon things will be even better."

How does Iacocca rate according to the EPOD Theory? He has outstanding high energy (E). His language was extremely persuasive (P), very much on target for his dealers, his managers, stockholders, and the general public. Certain members of the press saw his language as puffery, but they were not the primary constituency he was trying to persuade. His optimism (O) was outstanding. In addition, he used strong discipline (D) in timing his forecasts and then following through. EPOD at its best.

How Do You Feel about You?

If you hold a leadership position, how you feel about yourself determines how other people in the environment feel because you inject either positivity or negativity into that environment.

The charismatic Sam Walton, founder of Wal-Mart, operated with an unbridled level of optimism, which had a pass-through effect on his executives, managers, and in fact most of his employees. Remember that he called employees "associates." Using his optimistic style he sought their advice and input on tough issues, then complimented them when ideas worked. As a leader in a company, association, religious congregation, or your own home, your optimism is crucial; **our society is beset by the press with a heavy air of negativism.** At the close of the 1970s, during the height of unemployment (about 10 percent), the press began circulating stories that stated, "Unemployment is now at 10 percent, the highest total since the Great Depression."

Yet who reported that we were still employing 90 percent of our employable workforce? Moreover, the comparison with the Great Depression was unfounded. During the 1930s, 27 percent of the American workforce was unemployed. You can't compare 10 percent with what happened in 1930. No one mentioned that no industrialized nation with a population of more than 200 million, except the United States, has been able to continually employ 90 percent or more of its available labor.

Pessimism permeates the news media, and society must seek it and enjoy it, or the media would not continue to offer it. I believe if the refrigerator were invented today, the teaser for the evening news would be, "A great calamity has befallen the ice-making industry." It seems easier to be pessimistic than optimistic in today's society. We have so much, though we value it so little. Many of us who live in a world of abundance feel compelled to cry about what we do not have.

Your customers and your staff are subjected to heavy doses of media negativism. Your deep-felt optimism is a badly needed breath of fresh air and a key ingredient for success.

Examine this next case study. In a sea of negativity, it is important to search out facts, then play on the stories of those positive issues that stimulate and make us feel proud.

Case #112: Optimism Is More Than Dreaming.

> "Some people look at things that seem impossible and say, 'Why?' I look at things and say, 'Why not?'"
> —*Various sources*

On May 8, 1945, every bell in every church and city building in Palermo, Italy, rang continuously from early morning to noon. It was the day that Germany officially surrendered to the Allies to signify the end of their participation in World War II.

Many believe, however, the bell ringing was to welcome the birth of Giovanni (Nino) Vitale. Those who know him best believe this bell-ringing indoctrination gave spark to Nino's unbridled optimism.

Nino is the C.E.O. of Temo, Inc., currently the largest manufacturer of thermal sunrooms in the United States. He guides the activities of over 250 employees and 140 dealer organizations, the combination of which manufacture, fabricate, and install this popular alternative to conventional family rooms for American home owners. Nino and Temo have received many kudos. Beyond engineering know-how, a unique product, and a marketing arm that is arguably the leader in the sunroom industry, Nino's ability to see the future and respond to paradigm shifts has been uncanny. One of his associates said recently, "Nino has dreams but so do others; however, Nino builds on his dreams and makes them reality."

Let's take a step back. How did Nino get from May 8, 1945, in Palermo, Italy, one of four children in an agricultural family, to where he is today?

His father died when he was two months old. He dropped out of school after the eighth grade and at the age of fourteen left home to earn a living. His first job was making cappuccinos at a beach resort. Ever the diligent worker even at menial tasks, his early work history as a pasta maker, factory worker, and his stint of two years in the Italian Army would seem to have little to do with becoming a CEO in a large American company.

In 1968, at the age of twenty-three, he came to the United States with a few hundred dollars, the opportunity for a job as a carpenter's helper, and the inability to speak English. This doesn't sound like much of a foundation for starting a business, yet one year later he and his friends started a small business in the basement of a home, packaging aluminum skirting for mobile homes, a process now called manufactured housing.

Imagine: you are twenty-four, you are still trying to learn the language of your newly adopted country, and you have no background or history in running an American business. Then someone decides to take you to an international exposition for the manufactured housing industry. You see a product that has a much different application, and you optimistically see it in use for the wall and roof area of sunrooms. *Voila!* The dream is in place.

Now comes the hard part for most of us. How do you sell your dream to others who only speak and understand the English language? The answer, of course. is to go to night school and learn English. But what about understanding American sales and marketing? Nino says that the first time he heard the word "marketing," he identified it with people in Italy who shop each day for their groceries at the "market."

Are you getting the picture? Here is a man who thirty years later would own a 130,000-square-foot manufacturing facility, employ hundreds, and influence thousands. He will become the number-one marketer in his industry, and he was from the very beginning. and remains today, undaunted when matching effort to task.

Many who started to work for him in 1971 when the new company was formed are still with him. Unquestionably, Nino Vitale's energy (E), when applied to his dream and fueled by his level of optimism (O), equals unbridled success.

Through his efforts, hundreds of companies have learned the distribution and marketing techniques that have enabled them to become clones of the Temo system. A shining example is a company in Tidewater, Virginia, named Melani Brothers. Two young men from Pittsburgh—without business, marketing, or sales experience—emulated the concepts taught by Nino and in turn became the largest sunroom dealer in the United States. As Ray and Ron Melani tell the story, from their original inquiry they were guided by Nino via phone through the engineering, design, and installation of their first sunroom. They quickly latched on to this optimistic mentor and subsequently built a business that is still a marvel in terms of its uniqueness and dominance in their marketplace. They run a company with offices in two cities and ninety employees. At the root of their success, they believe, beyond a unique product and a powerful marketing technique live the passion and optimism of Nino Vitale.

Recently, Nino was honored when asked to speak at Central Michigan University. He is often nonplused at those who regard his success story as unique. In his message to the students and faculty of that university, he stated, "My greatest education was simply coming to, then being part of the American dream. This country unfolds its arms to people like me without education. Think of how much greater the opportunity is for someone who was born here and has an education."

Converting the Vitale dream to reality had three cornerstones. The first is, be sure you have a system. One of Nino's favorite expressions is, "The system reigns supreme." Of course, adhering to this system requires discipline (D).

The second cornerstone is having a passion for what you are doing. In Nino's philosophy, the passion drives the energy (E).

The final cornerstone is caring about the people who work for you as well as those who buy your product. In Nino's world, being persuasive (P) is measured by the degree of caring. He often quotes a familiar, yet seldom-used concept for business, "People don't care how much you know until they know how much you care."

Fighting the Blahs, Blues, and Depression

I am sometimes asked, "Do you ever get depressed?" My answer is, "Yes and no." Yes, like all other human beings I get depressed. In fact, I have never met a human being who did not get depressed sometimes. The no part occurs because I do not permit myself to stay depressed. When depression is evident, I don't allow myself the option of maintaining it. I choose not to tolerate it. Most depression, except the extreme clinical type, doesn't simply come; it comes, then stays with your approval.

Dr. Wayne Dyer, in his book *Erroneous Zones*, stresses that we can choose our emotions. Much of what we call depression or being down is a choice, except in severe cases of manic depression or instances of bipolarity.

The Fallacy of Believing Things Are Going To Get Better

While I maintain an optimistic outlook I never believe simply that things will get better. This belief is not contrary to maintaining an optimistic outlook. Rather, it is a stepping stone for action. I don't believe that things will just naturally get better by themselves: **It is up to me, and I can take action to makes things get better.**

If you are selling nine products and the market dries up in three of them, you could lose a third of your business. However, you can invest more energy in the sales of the remaining six products by believing that they are going to make up the difference.

> The resolve to make things better stems not from a whimsical type of optimism based on hopes and wishes, but from an action-oriented one that says, "I can make things better."

Optimism is a choice. Pessimism is a choice. Much depression is a choice. So too, happiness is a choice. Abraham Lincoln once said, "Most people are about as happy as they make their minds up to be." Keep in mind the statement was made by one of the most reviled presidents ever to serve the United States, a man who suffered severe depression, stood for the rights of others despite a lack of support on both sides of many issues, and a man who when he was assassinated earned a line in his obituary stating, "He died more loathed than loved."

The Typical Approach to Each Day

Many people approach each new day lying in bed dreading the alarm buzzer. Then it goes off. If they stayed up too late the night before, had too much to eat, or overexerted themselves, they get up stiff and sore. They drag themselves into the bathroom and groan. In his book *Inside America*, Louis Harris writes that most people are unhappy about the way they look and dress. They do not like the way their hair looks, or they see themselves as too short, too fat, too tall, or too thin.

Whatever the reason, many people are not happy when starting the day, which is **the most important time of the day to generate optimism.**

The greatest audience in the world does not consist of your employees, your customers, or the people you have to report to; the greatest audience in the world is the audience of one: you. If you start with an optimistic view and tell the audience of one (you) what kind of day it will be, your optimism will permeate your relationships and business environment. However, this approach to life takes practice. Generating optimism is an exercise for your mind, just as working out at the health club is exercise for your body. You can develop bigger biceps by lifting weights; you can increase your level of optimism by lifting your spirits.

Start Your Day with Optimism

If you would like to experiment, try some of these suggestions and measure whether your "O" factor has increased:

- When you get up in the morning, try to avoid reading the front page of the newspaper. Start with the lighter sections such as the sports page or lifestyle, and maybe the comics. Turn to the front page last, where you will get a heavy analysis of what's wrong with the world from an institution steeped in negativity.
- As a daily exercise, when you rise and start to shave or put on your makeup, instead of contemplating what has gone wrong in your life and in your company, and all the things that may go wrong today, choose to acknowledge how far you have come in life—your accomplishments—and how this is going to be a great day.

Years ago I learned this simple exercise: when I get up in the morning, the first thing I say to myself out loud is, "This is going to be a great day." Then I say, "This day belongs to me, no one can take it away." I tell myself I am going to have a great day, because **my real job each day is to feel good about me.**

I do not run through the litany of everything that happened the day before—what I liked or didn't like. I do not deal in the long history of what could be seen as negative things that have happened in my life. If some of those thoughts emerge, I view each negative event as the positive motivator of where I am headed today.

I attempt to bring my optimism to those with whom I will come in contact today. Before I get to the office and encounter my employees and my clients, **I remember I can carry with me and transmit optimism all day.** If I catch my optimism slipping, I repeat my special affirmation:

> "I am a unique and precious being created by God for very special purposes. I am ever doing the best I can. I am ever growing in love and awareness."

Then I recite a version for others, because they are unique and precious beings created by God for special purposes, and they are ever doing the best they can. When another person offends you or says something that is inconsistent with your value system, especially remember, "They are ever doing the best they can." **If they could do better, they would.**

Get into Action. Optimism is ignited by action. If your coworkers or staff are pessimistic, accept the challenge of remaining optimistic. Use centering techniques or silent affirmations.

When you hear employees say, "This won't work," or "I can't do this," offer them an encouraging, optimistic message: "Sure it can, and you're just the person to make it work." Make sure that your employees offer the same type of message to customers.

Create Long-Term Customers

Optimism, like persuasive language, helps develop and maintain long-term customers. Let's return to Alice at the service department of the auto parts company. A second customer calls. After gathering the appropriate information, Alice's response is, "Bring it in and we'll get to work on it."

A similar response is *not* offered by the competitor up the street. Customers are likely to hear:

> "We don't really handle that here. . . ."
> "If you will read 'Provision #19A' of your warranty . . . ,"
> "We can send it down to our plant in New Jersey."

or anything else that conveys the message, "We don't really want to serve you after the sale. We're afraid you are going to squander our time and lower our profitability."

The optimistic company, headed by an optimistic manager, relishes the opportunity to secure another satisfied customer, because having additional contact with customers contributes to the development of long-term relationships. The optimistic manager knows that **by offering a high degree of service, the probability is raised that others will become dependent upon that service.** The optimistic manager looks forward to opportunities to offer the message, "You can depend on us."

A Taste of Outlandish Optimism

Perhaps the best example of optimism I have heard comes from Senator Bob Murphey of Nacogdoches, Texas. He was waiting for me in the back of a room, dressed in western attire: Stetson hat, string tie, and fancy boots. He said:

> Dave, I heard you talkin' 'bout optimism, and I wanna tell you 'bout the most optimistic man I know, my cousin Calvin Lee Rose.
>
> Calvin Lee was running for political office. He went out and picked up the voter registration polls and put them over the sun visor of his car. That's how he found the people he wanted to talk to.
>
> He searched out this here woman's house, and he went up and knocked on the door. The woman come to the door and he

swept off his hat and said, "Good morning, ma'am. My name is Calvin Lee Rose, and I'm a-runnin' for assistant deputy dog catcher in this town and I would surely appreciate your vote." He then put his Stetson back on.

The woman said, "Calvin Lee Rose, I know you and I know your whole blessed family, and none of you are any dang good. You been divorced three times, you drink whiskey, play cards, and you hung around with loose women most of your life. If you were the only-est man left on the face of the earth, I would not vote for you, and if the buzzards was comin' to look over your body if you dropped dead I would not shoo 'em. And if you don't get off my porch I'm a-goin' to get my husband's 16-gauge shotgun and fill your posterior with lead."

Calvin Lee swept his Stetson off and said to her, "I thank you, ma'am."

He left and got back in his car, removed the voter registration card from the sun visor, searched down until he found that woman's name, held the place with his thumb, removed the pencil from behind his ear, wet the pencil on his tongue, and wrote after her name, "doubtful."

Points:	[0]	[1]	[2]	[3]
	Never	Occasionally	Frequently	Always

1. Do I start each day with an optimistic self-affirmation such as, "This is going to be a great day," or "I am looking forward to today"?
2. Do I understand that most statistics have nothing to do with me, that it is my determination and attitude which affects the outcome of situations?
3. Do I consciously work at projecting optimism to others?
4. Do I minimize the time spent worrying about competition or other issues I cannot change?
5. Do I avoid 'losing heart' when my ideas are subject to negativity or rejected?
6. Do I regard 'objections' as a sign of interest?
7. Do I accept compliments about myself graciously and frequently compliment others sincerely?
8. Do I believe that the world is essentially full of 'good people'?
9. Do I believe that if things are going properly then I can influence them to continue?
10. Do I consciously accept that the mind does not know the difference between the real and the imaginary, and that I can choose to feel great today?

If you score 15 or less, work on developing an optimistic outlook.

Over 20 indicates you are above average yet need more frequency of optimistic feelings.

A score of 24 to 28 puts you in an elite group (probably less than 10 percent of the population) with the potential to influence others.

EPOD Tactics

- The strategy to instill positivity and optimism starts with the abandonment of old ideas, limits, and problem-solving methods, and the adoption of a new language that eliminates negativity and value judging. It requires that you develop a new attitude and a language of optimism for you and your company.
- Often, we are critical of people who are negative. While I have never been criticized for being overly positive, I do find that many people regard this as cockiness.
- Try to be creative as opposed to critical whenever you attempt to communicate issues that require correction. If you return from a trip and your furniture has more dust on it than you'd like, instead of being critical, write, "I love you" in the dust.
- If you experience anger towards someone, record your feelings on a CD or cassette. On playback the next day, if you are still angry, add new feelings and subtract that which no longer applies. Keep the recording in your positivity library. This short exercise reduces the energy given to anger and helps you get on with the business of living.
- Acknowledge that if things are going too good, it does not mean that something bad is going to happen.
- Take full responsibility for your own happiness.
- Avoid phrases such as, "Look what you made me do," or "If you hadn't done this, everything would have worked out fine."
- Do not allow yourself to be pessimistically influenced by media statistics, economic downturns, or unemployment.
- One of two circumstances probably governs the business calls you receive: (1) the caller is already doing business with you and wants to do more, or (2) the caller is interested in buying something from you or is seeking your services for the first time.

    Make sure that the phone is used as a tool and not as a weapon. Have the person answering your phone
    ○ Smile before they speak to the caller
    ○ Speak slowly and clearly

- Use an upbeat and enthusiastic voice
- Make that caller feel important
* Accept yourself exactly as you are, with your exact circumstances. That does not mean that you are going to accept your way of life and not grow; rather, accept yourself and love yourself as you are.
* Avoid devaluating or putting yourself down. You are a unique creation with the capability to shine. Never take great risks with what God gave you: your body and your mind.

CHAPTER 4
Discipline

"The major and measurable difference in the performance of most high achievers and top managers is how they choose to deal with unpleasant or less desirable tasks."
—*Dave Yoho*, Managing Yourself & Others

The fourth element of EPOD is **Discipline**, which frequently involves **doing many of the things you don't like to do, yet doing most of them well**. The lack of discipline is probably the greatest single barrier to high-performance management or simply getting what we want out of life. If we don't discipline ourselves, then society or nature usually will. The undisciplined way of life usually ends up in disappointment, chaos, and inconsistent achievement levels, and frequently downright unhappiness.

Today, many people have a desire for immediate gratification. Young people often immediately want the benefits of being adults. New entrants into the labor force want to rise faster than their experience and abilities dictate. Executives choose shortcuts to acquire wealth. Too often, the inability to delay gratification through self-discipline has strong consequences, ultimately destroying dreams and goals.

Case #6: The Discipline to Gather Knowledge

C. Ray Johnson, the past president of Coachmen Industries (a major recreational vehicle manufacturer in the United States), went on to become president of a division of Kaufman and Broad and ultimately put together his first leveraged buyout before the age of forty. Effectively managing public corporations; being responsible to accountants, lawyers, the SEC, stockholders, and thousands of employees; setting up plants; buying and selling real estate; and dealing with myriad advertising and public relations responsibilities might seem impossible when you consider that Johnson has only a high school education. Yet he may be one of the most educated people I know. What he lacked in formal education he made up for with his exercise of discipline.

Johnson, a client and friend, read almost every major business book published. He maintained a library of business cassettes, CDs, and videotapes that rivaled many retail stores. A disciplined reader and listener, he had playback equipment in his car and office and throughout his home, and he maintained a self-designed daily educational program. His follow-through on new ideas was unsurpassed.

Within his busy schedule he attended many seminars annually. He was an early member of the Young Presidents Organization, the Sales Executive Club of New York, and many other organizations that gave him an opportunity to network and enhance his knowledge of business.

Johnson's ability to pick apart a financial statement, analyze internal operating conditions, forecast, and accomplish turnarounds was the envy of many business executives. He ranks with the most accomplished people I have cited in publications and speeches, and I always refer to him when I talk about the law of compensating balances. Prior to his retirement, he wrote a marvelous book on corporate management, *C.E.O. Logic* (Career Press 1998), in which he chronicled the attributes that lead to management success.

Case #55: Using Discipline to Keep Your Head When All about You Are Losing Theirs

In 1978, when Paul Franks moved to the Hilton Head resort community in South Carolina, the Hilton Head—based Sea Pines Real Estate Company was in its heyday. Franks had sold his oil distribution business in Atlanta and, after considering other options, decided to start a new career and sell real estate—something he had never done before.

Franks joined a seventeen-person sales organization and rose rapidly. By 1980 he was the vice president of residential sales. In 1981, a banner year for the company, he became vice president of real estate, directing fifty salespeople who broke all records for real estate sales in the state of South Carolina.

Then a series of reorganizations severely tested Franks's optimism and discipline. Over the next six years the entire Sea Pines Plantation and Resort was sold, restructured, and reorganized. It fell under the control of seven different management groups, all of whom developed crippling cash flow, credit, and credibility problems. Through various policy changes, Franks's own office was moved seven times. By mid-1987, a trustee had to be appointed to operate the bankrupt entity.

I had been a consultant for Sea Pines prior to the decline and owned a vacation home there. I knew most of the top management and witnessed firsthand the degeneration and demotivation of staff relationships. Although my contract terminated when the original owners sold out, I continued to follow this organization with great interest. Despite horrendous circumstances, bad press, and low morale in other divisions of the company, the real estate division, under Franks, continued to expand, prosper, and even set new records during this tumultuous period.

Consider the discipline of Paul Franks, who attended executive conferences weekly and was routinely exposed to bad news, reports of insolvency, rapid management changes, and lack of consistency. Despite this, he returned each time to stimulate, inspire, and motivate his sales staff. Paul Franks's division expanded to double its size, with sales figures that made it the largest real estate company in South Carolina.

At lunch one day I asked him how he pulled it off. He said that it took great discipline to stick to his plan, which he wrote, rewrote, and faithfully followed. Here were the basics of the eight-step plan:

- Retain your best salespeople and always affirm and nurture them.
- Manage the money so as to never miss paying a commission check.
- Pay all real estate division bills promptly and advise all vendors monthly.
- Be truthful with and don't disappoint the purchasers.
- Mentally divorce yourself from the company problems; perceive the real estate division as separate and independent.
- Don't bring bad news back from a meeting, and don't permit negativity in your division.
- Show your staff and salespeople how to effectively deal with controversial publicity and rumors, and be the role model.
- Forecast reasonable increases monthly and annually, and reach them.

Since its reorganization in 1987, Sea Pines has been owned by residents of the resort community. Thanks to the unwavering success and financial strength of the real estate division it has attained solidarity in its financial and administrative structure.

Franks never gave up, and the majority of his staff responded positively to his discipline. To paraphrase Rudyard Kipling:

"If you can keep your head when all about you are losing theirs," brother, you've got discipline.

A Crucial Business Element

Discipline or the lack of it plays a major role for a business and the individuals within that business. For example, salespeople seldom like to prepare their call reports, complete paperwork or make cold calls. Yet these three tasks are basic to the sales role.

Without diligence and discipline the salesperson will often abandon ongoing efforts and experience failure. Moreover, sales managers are frequently limited in enforcement capabilities. Attempts to force, intimidate, or cajole staffs may work, but for only a brief period. The key is for the salesperson to understand the importance of these less glamorous tasks and exhibit a high level of energy in their completion.

Many sales organizations fail to recognize that most salespeople would rather call on a familiar face than solicit a new account. Professionals offering services would rather have someone call them than make new sales calls. Salespeople tend to be comfortable doing business with certain types of people or organizations and avoiding others, regardless of sales potential, and most salespeople would rather make a new sale than deal with a service issue.

Yet individuals who employ discipline recognize the value of completing less glamorous tasks, because they realize such activity will help them reach their goals that much sooner.

My consulting experience has shown me that most major corporations are highly structured, controlled by policies, and have business plans. Smaller companies and entrepreneurs seldom use any of these controls. In many cases the owners of small businesses don't exert the discipline necessary to undertake such plans or do the necessary follow-through. Even when these companies retain an outside consultant to prepare a plan, they frequently don't follow it; the discipline to follow-through is often lacking.

In large corporations, preparing forecasts, budgets, financial controls, management plans, goals, and quotas are the responsibilities of managers who are then assessed and evaluated periodically.

The disciplines that are built into larger companies are often lacking in small businesses. Entrepreneurs who do achieve financial success manage to shorten their work load, heighten their productivity, and profitability, and run a more efficient business by exerting higher levels of discipline than their contemporaries.

Fundamental Disciplines

In business, the lack of discipline frequently leads to failure.

Most successful managers concede that there are two businesses within every business. The first is managing the business, profession, or trade as well as marketing, selling, and developing the products or services. The second business is administering budgets, personnel selection, control and development, maintaining cash flow, monitoring return on investment and return on assets deployed, goal setting, forecasting, tax and estate planning, and more. When businesses fail, the owners often had part one working well, yet never quite had a handle on part two.

Having knowledge of a trade or profession is not the same as running a business. The skilled auto mechanic who wants to open up his own auto repair service shop may not be qualified to do so. The talented lawyer in a prestigious law firm who sets off on his own may not have the discipline or drive necessary to be successful, though his capability as a lawyer is excellent.

The business of running a business requires much more than being skilled at providing services. It involves meeting a payroll, being able to make wise purchasing decisions, maintaining a positive cash flow, ensuring profitability, making hiring and firing decisions, and a host of other responsibilities. My old friend and client, Norman Kailian, the now-retired president of Appleby Window Systems, was once asked the greatest weakness he had to overcome in building his multidivisioned business. He said, "If I was doing it again, I would learn to hire better and slower, and when it wasn't working to fire quicker." Discipline in business often requires going back to basics: learning from your errors and making decisions logically instead of emotionally.

Here is another example of how discipline, or the lack of it, affects smaller businesses. Many business people consider it difficult or impossible to **learn how to read a balance sheet and income statement**. Many business owners don't know how and won't take the time or exert the discipline to learn. Ergo, they are seldom prepared for the decisions they may need to make or how to react to circumstances which occur that require change.

Case #206: The O.D.D. Choice— Optimism, Discipline, Diversity

"The only limit to our realization of tomorrow will be our doubts of today."
—*Franklin Delano Roosevelt*

Did you ever feel that you had to walk the balance beam between separate worlds, that your decisions were being influenced by two different cultures or disciplines, thus making goals and direction complicated?

David Moore is the product of a hardworking middle-class family who strove to have their children get great educations and become achievers. High achievements in high school led David to prestigious honors at Amherst College, followed by a degree from Harvard Business School. His father and two uncles ran the family business, and did their share to provide the potential for a great education for all the nieces and nephews.

Shortly after graduating from Harvard, the grandfather who founded the business and the uncle who ran it as president passed away suddenly. Unfortunate economics sent the company into a tailspin. David Moore, with his accumulated skills, education, and potential in the corporate world, had to make a decision. Having already been exposed to major corporations and issues of Wall Street, and with the potential for a management position at one of several Fortune 500 companies, David elected to buy the company that had been the basis of his family's success. The company engaged in the sale and application of unique products used in the remodeling business. In 1992, while suffering through the difficulties of reorganization, David did what many would have considered a difficult choice. He bought and became the sole owner of Garden State Brickface, headquartered in New Jersey.

His ability to absorb detail, create and administer a unique business plan, and select and manage the people who would run this company did not pay big dividends immediately. However, through diligence, hard work, and discipline, he turned the New Jersey company into one of the country's largest and most efficient specialty remodeling companies.

Then to make his dream true for others, he created an ESOP (Employee Stock Option Plan) for his employees. Without any investment on their part, the employees now own a significant part of the company. Through David Moore's discipline, each year this company has grown in volume and stature in the business community. He is also chairman of Sonostar Ventures, an investment firm in Chappaqua, New York, which he cofounded a number of years ago with a fellow Amherst and Harvard classmate, Greg Kiernan. Moore has also worked at putting various merger and acquisition deals together, including Metropolitan Life's 1996 sale of its Century 21 Real Estate Corporation to HFS, Inc., later Cendant. His boardroom stints include time both with public and nonpublic corporations as well as with several major charities.

Yet, there's more. While David Moore is able through discipline to separate the efforts of two dissimilar aspects of his business career, he also became involved with an unusual avocation. Almost unbelievably he took on the role of a standup comedian while in his mid-forties. In a process that psychologists often refer to as neoteny (aging while maintaining childlike practices), David added a new dimension to his already successful business career. Over the years he has performed his standup comedy at the country's premier comedy clubs, including Caroline's on Broadway and the Friars Club in New York City, and The

Improv in Los Angeles. He approaches this avocation the way other corporate types play golf or climb mountains—somewhat addictively. Making time for this avocation between running his own business and serving on various corporate boards is complicated.

Moore says the business side of his life gives him energy for comedy, and vice versa. He is writing a book (*Leading with Laughter*) and has entered the speaking circuit, advising executives on how to bring a sense of humor into the workplace.

David Moore is an ideal example of the fulfillment of the American dream, and moreover he personifies the EPOD Theory. He approaches, then attacks all business issues with high energy (E). He is equally at home in the boardroom of Wall Street companies and the offices of entrepreneurial businesses because he has a persuasive style (P) that convinces others that he truly understands their issues and problems. He is optimistic to a fault. Where others see failure, fault and negativity, David Moore tends to see the bright side. Who but an optimist would take a Harvard education and an extremely intellectual persona, stand in a Brooks Brothers suit among other standup comedians who tend to be underdressed and frequently foul-mouthed, and win the day? Moore is beyond optimistic (O); he knows he has audience appeal.

Finally, beyond his many skills, David Moore has the discipline (D) to understand the difference in the stage persona versus the duties and style of the CEO and is always cautious about separating them. He says running a major business and guiding the actions of others in the pursuit of net profit and a positive balance sheet is no laughing matter.

The Discipline to Give Up Tasks

Most entrepreneurs and managers tie up their time with trivial tasks that they don't need to be handling. Continuous growth in a small business eventually demands that someone else opens the mail and orders supplies rather than the entrepreneur. Likewise, within an organization, if you are a manager or a division head, you have to continuously assess what you can let go of. Have the discipline to delegate and pass off menial tasks and activities that have been part of your routine and concentrate on more important things.

Managers who deal in too much trivia cannot be effective interacting with their employees. Even if you are the best at purchasing supplies, assign that task to someone else. That other person may never do the job as effectively as you. However, assigning someone to handle purchases frees you to investigate changes necessary to your business, or to make better long-term plans. Regular reviews, mentoring, and appraisals will aid you in having confidence in your assistant or department head.

Monthly, create a list of three trivial tasks you will give up. Once you accomplish these, move on to three more. David Moore, our last case example, hired an efficiency consultant to guide him through a similar process, thus enabling him to acquire new businesses and create divisions in his existing company.

Examine the circumstances of this next case, which are more common than you might think. However, the outcome is uncommon.

Case #9: Inheriting the Family Business.

> "Discipline is a key ingredient for those who may otherwise never get to know how great they can be."

The late Peter Heaney became the president of Skaggs-Walsh, a large fuel oil dealer in metropolitan New York, upon the death of his father. With an established staff and management, he faced the pressures of running a business in a highly competitive market. The problems of a constantly changing customer base, increasing volume, and decreasing profits seemed more than this twenty-two-year-old could handle.

Heaney, a shy man with an excellent business education from St. John's University, felt great frustration in attempting to direct this once-viable business that was now in decline. Within two years he added 105 pounds, developed a three-pack-per-day cigarette habit, and began downing a couple of martinis at lunch to cope with the daily pressures.

When Heaney's company became our client, we examined all of these conditions and suggested the following: that he develop a new training discipline for his salespeople, change his marketing thrust, and restructure his organization. We also requested that he participate on service calls, including inquiries for new oil customers and those seeking estimates for new equipment.

Any one of these changes would have been a considerable task for the average individual. The latter suggestion was antithesis to this young man's behavioral structure. However, with the support of his wife Joan and a prewritten marketing plan, he set out to both restructure the company and learn the basics from the ground up.

The initial resistance from his own salespeople, coupled with his lack of understanding of the sales role, presented extreme challenges. Yet within less than a year the following had happened:

- Peter installed a training regimen for his salespeople, for which he had become the pilot. For three out of the next twelve months he was the top producer in his sales organization.
- He wrote a new computer program and developed the software to implement the marketing plan, gaining a reputation in his market territory as a "leader in sales and service."
- His prices were not the lowest, yet dozens of customers wrote with comments about the efficiency and effectiveness of his company.

In his own words, without discipline he would have given up after one month. It took much longer than that to get the whole process working, but Heaney stayed on course. Subsequently, he sent my company this letter:

"We attempted to follow the guidelines which you recommended as closely as possible, and this became our greatest profit year. As you will see in the attached chart, we actually doubled the number of accounts.

"As an added benefit, our bank (Chemical) was equally impressed. Last year our line of credit was $1,350,000, and this year we have reduced our borrowing to $750,000.

"In addition, we now have on deposit over $400,000 and in the same period last year the balance on our loan was $550,000.

"I am almost afraid to ask—what do we do now?"

Peter F. Heaney
President
Skaggs-Walsh, Inc.
College Point, NY

Peter became a shining example of discipline. He became a svelte (one hundred pounds lighter), nonsmoking, non-drinking business executive who played tennis twice a week. He acquired several additional companies equal in size to his first and received an honorary doctorate from St. John's University. He exemplified the statement:

> The disciplined individual masters the art of engaging in that which they prefer not to do.

Redesign your business environment to accommodate the customer as well as the employee. Create a methodology for each task, from answering the phone to responding to the most complex problem. The methods will be part of what we call "the system." Everyone can be taught "the system" and encouraged to practice it and pass it on. In each office the guiding message is:

"THE SYSTEM REIGNS SUPREME"

Here is a partial conversion list that we frequently give to clients with established businesses. Some of these apply to small businesses. Most apply to managers in companies of any size. The key element is whether the general manager or CEO will exercise the discipline necessary to see that these ideas are fulfilled.

- Stop opening the mail (and don't replace this with hovering over the desk of the person who ultimately does).
- Create a business plan each year at least two months before the old year ends.
- Take a course at a local university or junior college to better understand or get updated on current accounting and tax issues.
- Stay in touch with your customers. If they normally come to your place of business, use a simple two- or three-question customer satisfaction survey. Use telephone follow-up if you service or sell to them at their home or place of business. Ask for and get updating (in all cases) for address, phone, fax, and e-mail. Send something regularly through those means to let the customer know you care.
- Create standard appraisal formats for all employees/associates. Grade them in ten to twelve categories (scale of 1 [low] to 10 [high]). Review these quarterly.
- Delegate often, become a mentor and a supervisor.

Here is the crash course in disciplined economics. Most of it applies to individuals and businesses alike. Start with the primary rules. If you master this, you will never grow broke:

- Spend less money than you take in.
- Don't pay interest if you can avoid it.
- Buy at the longest terms your vendor will offer, sell at the shortest terms if possible. This creates healthy cash flow.
- Use your balance sheet, not your checkbook, to determine cash available.
- Don't purchase inventory, equipment, advertising, or similar services on impulse. Use a budget forecast plan.
- Never permit desire to overbalance negotiation.
- Regulate your purchases to leverage your cash. If you can, buy on "statement." Purchases made in the last few days

of a month may not require payment for an additional thirty days.
- Send a letter to all your vendors, large and small, requesting prompt payment discounts. If they don't already offer them, first state your satisfaction with their product or service, then indicate your interest in saving by improving your and their business relations.
- If you are paying your staff on a weekly basis, change it to a biweekly basis. You write twenty-six less checks per person per year, improve your cash flow, and reduce the accounting entries.

Discipline: Internal or External

Discipline also means preparing for and adjusting to changes in your marketplace, the economy, and public tastes. Discipline means not permitting others to convince you that things are unworkable. It may require avoiding those people or situations which create doubt, lower your integrity or morals, or ask you to question your discipline.

The discipline that you display has a strong impact on your associates and customers. Almost everything you do in life and business will be affected by your discipline or lack of it.

> If you do not exercise discipline yourself, society, nature, or customers create issues that ultimately will.

If you overeat, your cardiovascular system will make you pay. If you smoke, your lungs will suffer damage. If you don't exercise discipline in your business, you may fail. If you spend more than you take in, you will be disciplined by banks, creditors, and the IRS, plus you will experience difficulty making payroll regularly.

Discipline Yourself or Be Disciplined

Prior to speaking at a conference one morning I tested the sound system after returning from jogging. A woman came by

and noticed that I was in my sweat suit, headband, and running shoes and inquired, "Oh, you're a runner?" I responded, "Yes, since I was twenty-eight years old."
She said, "You must love it."
"No," I said, "it is drudgery. I have been rained on, hosed down, and bitten by dogs. I have had twisted ankles and have endured aches, pains, and muscle pulls."
"Then why do you do it?" she asked.
"Because the discipline of jogging five days a week keeps my cardiovascular system in top shape." My pulse rate is 52 standing and 48 resting. This a major factor that has enabled me to complete my demanding schedule annually.

Discipline to Lose Weight

Let's say you are forty-seven pounds overweight and would like to lose that weight. Don't go on a diet, because starting a diet is not an effective application of the EPOD Theory. Instead draw upon your discipline capabilities and cut out one thing at a time. Harold Waller removed butter from his diet for twenty-one days and lost some weight. Then he began another twenty-one-day cycle and removed white bread from his diet. Then meat. In the fifth twenty-one-day period he limited his alcohol consumption to two glasses of wine per week. After 105 days, he lost a total of twenty-five pounds and began a new regimen to maintain his new lower weight.

You can lose weight, and you don't have to go on some kind of earth-shattering diet. If you are clinically obese and have been under a doctor's care, this doesn't apply to you.

If you have average health and happen to be overweight, cut just one item from your diet for a twenty-one-day period. For starters, try butter. You will lose weight.

Reachable and Rewarding. Discipline is acquired, it is not something with which you are born. Ask yourself what is the greatest skill that you bring to your work or profession. Is it stamina, endurance, leadership, believability, interpersonal skills, loyalty, dedication? Whatever it is, I guarantee you were not born with it; you acquired it as a result of life experiences that taught you the true value and need of whatever skill or discipline you developed.

So too, the successful person and the successful business adopt those disciplines that enable them to survive and prosper.

Discipline is the make-or-break component of the EPOD Theory.

In alliance with energy, persuasiveness, and optimism, the business and the individual possessing discipline have all the tools for potential success. In the absence of discipline, all the energy, persuasiveness and optimism in the world may not be enough.

Points: [0] [1] [2] [3]
Never Occasionally Frequently Always

1. Do I create a plan for my new business direction or lifestyle change?
2. Do I consciously work on changing habits which are not in my best interest?
3. Have I been successful in ridding myself of habits which are not in my best interest, i.e. overeating, smoking, drinking?
4. Do I use part of each day to learn something new?
5. If I am required to perform an undesirable task do I bring high energy to the task?
6. Do I research the breakdowns in my interaction with others to determine a source and corrective process?
7. Do I maintain a positive attitude during periods of change?
8. Do I set long range goals, break them down into groups and track them on a regular basis?
9. When I am partially successful in goal completion do I maintain commitment to the project?
10. Do I work well with others who have behaviors or habits of which I do not approve?

10 to 15 indicates a low level of discipline.
16 to 20 indicates a moderate level of discipline.
21 to 24 indicates an effective level of discipline.
25 or higher is excellent.

EPOD Tactics

- **Nature helps, but it's nurture that counts most.** Society continues to debate what makes one individual successful while another fails: nature or nurture? I've seen enough cases to believe it's mostly nurture. If average individuals exert the proper level of discipline, then they will become successful.
- Plan the next day's activities before leaving the office the night before. The simple discipline of scratching a note to yourself indicating the three or four priorities of the next workday alerts you to what you can look forward to.
- Warding off unmanageable stress in the workplace requires discipline:

   ➤ Not taking on a heavier workload than is reasonable
   ➤ Not making impractical time commitments and deadlines
   ➤ Not overreacting to people who seek confrontation or have incompatible behavior styles to yours
   ➤ Getting sufficient and regular feedback

- Make memos to yourself on everything you have done and will do, and what you are thinking.
- Acquire the habit of thoroughly reading something that is boring but beneficial.
- Take an extra five minutes to communicate with someone who you do not easily understand.
- Devote twenty-one days to effect a behavioral change in some area of interest to you.

CHAPTER 5
Create a Power Plan

"To know and not to do is not to know."
—*Zen proverb*

"Fifteen hundred and sixty weeks equal a career."
When I ask audiences what they will do with the next 1,560 weeks, after the puzzled looks and head scratching, someone usually figures out that 1,560 weeks equals 30 years.

The student about to enter college is saddled with a heavy responsibility: what courses to choose. The choices may affect how she makes her living and her happiness for decades to come. Yet she has only lived 25 percent of her expected life, most of it as a child.

Students and young professionals frequently stumble along on decisions made with limited input or knowledge. Many people choose to be lawyers, doctors, or engineers because of parental influence or because they have seen sixteen episodes of some sitcom.

While the path that leads people to their present occupation may be jagged, what's worse is that they usually continue further without a plan.

Before All, a Plan

When people read books such as this one, what they are frequently seeking is a magical formula that is going to make them successful. I have had clients who have an attitude of "Come in and make us rich." While that's not a bad idea, an attitude without a plan for fulfillment generally does not go very far. Turnarounds, raising profitability, and revised marketing/sales plans all require change and revision. So one of the first things we do is to formulate short- and long-range business plans.

Every change in business direction, ingrained attitude, or mind-set requires a plan. Some people who are forty pounds overweight want to lose that weight instantly. However, the weight was accumulated a pound at a time. Therefore, a more effective method is to take it off over a period of time—pound by pound. Effecting change in a business is best accomplished in the same manner.

If you want to modify or change your behavior, or that of others, work on one or two aspects of it at a time, not nine or ten.

Everyone Needs a Power Plan

Without a power plan you and/or your business are at risk as the circumstances around you change.

When a widow inherits her husband's estate, frequently, and regardless of the size of the estate, the assets are dissipated within seven to ten years. Many lottery winners who receive lump-sum payoffs don't fare much better.

Rooted in Reality. Most people who talk about achieving success don't spend much time actually planning for it by rearranging goals, priorities, and activities based on how their life is going to be. Entrepreneurs in particular are notorious nonplanners.

People who fantasize about having their own business frequently put great focus on being their own boss, and the amount of dollars that will roll in. Few envision the tremendous number of hours that are required to deal with suppliers, employees, creditors, business partners, and customers.

> When the reality of the efforts required to accomplish goals sets in, many people drop back to where they were, and thus little progress toward goals ever occurs.

Unless you have a power plan that enables you to structure your efforts, any decision you make will be made in the context of old behavior and habitual patterns. A written plan aids you in changing or modifying behaviors and staying focused.

Planning Always Helps

If you are an outgoing, aggressive type of person who wants to excel in customer service, you need a plan outlining ways you can let the customer rather than you be right. If you operate a business and sell one product now but wish to offer two new products, your transition will be much smoother if you devise a plan, however brief, that pinpoints how you intend to introduce the new product:

- The plan need not be more than one printed page.
- The plan can be in pros and cons or in outline form.
- The plan will logically carry you through the steps that you anticipate will be necessary to successfully market two more products.
- The plan is not etched in stone. As you implement initial steps, other parts of the plan may require modification.

From Plans to Simple Systems

When I construct a plan that represents a way of doing something that will be repeated, I often divide the plan into modules. For example, I developed a system of training called "Steps to a Sale." In this training I took every step in the sales cycle and broke each one into substeps, from the primary contact to the conclusion.

I then trained and coached my staff, and it became the method by which our sales system functioned. When a phone inquiry came in, the plan spelled out how it was to be handled: what would be said, the kind of form on which the inquiry would be recorded, and so forth.

I spent the time to plan and organize because without these tools my business wouldn't grow.

If you were to take an automobile trip of one thousand miles and you had never been to your destination before, you would take a road map. Yet people routinely get up each morning with no map and no plan, fully expecting to arrive somewhere.

Planning for Growth

Let's assume you recently started a small business. I ask you if the business is structured to do a million dollars annually, and you answer, "We are only planning to do $200,000 the first year." But if within five years you progress to sales of one or two million, how will you manage the company? Will you have a numbering sequence for your products or services, and a chart of accounts for your record-keeping control? Will you have a billing collection procedure? Will you have a method for handling cash? Approaching the realization of primary goals is not the time to let your guard down. It is the time to readdress your business plan to modify and augment it.

Too many entrepreneurs who get on a growth cycle can't deal with the success when it comes because they haven't planned for it.

Don't be concerned that your plan may be too premature:

- No plan is too premature.
- Any plan is better than no plan.
- All plans are subject to change.

The value of the planning process comes in the exercise of planning itself, not necessarily the validity of the plan, because you cannot know when you have the "perfect" plan anyway.

Checkbook Management Is Not Planning. Suppose you are a small business owner and you have made a decision to get involved in direct mail. You spend $15,000 on a direct mail campaign, and it goes bust. If the money for that campaign was part of operating capital, then you have put your business in jeopardy. But if it was financed with reserves held for this type of venture, you are still in relatively good shape.

Plan-oriented businesses build up such funds. Those without plans operate via checkbook management. This is characterized by the company or individual who sees a fair amount of money in the checkbook and then decides to make a purchase. This is a reckless way of managing finances.

On a personal basis, the checkbook manager is stung every time his car needs a major repair, or a home appliance gives out unexpectedly.

The checkbook manager frequently finds himself undertaking deficit spending and financial management using credit cards, so he is always paying the most for needed goods and services. He is dealing from a position of weakness.

When you accumulate assets you can usually buy things for less money. Suppliers are more inclined to do business with and offer more favorable terms to a company or individual who pays promptly. Banks are willing to give lower interest rates to customers with lots of assets. The person with the plan who acquires assets usually pays less and gets more.

Accumulating Principal. Part of an effective power plan is to have cash in the company. This approach allows you to take advantage of prompt payment discounts, buy in sufficient quantities to ensure the best price, and purchase off-season or during a supplier's downtime.

A company or individual is wise to accumulate cash as well as other liquid assets for other reasons. In an accelerating economy, replacement costs are usually higher than original costs. A piece of equipment purchased for $100,000 with seven or eight years' depreciation may have a book value of a few thousand dollars. When it is time to replace that equipment, it may cost $150,000 versus the $100,000 original investment. If you accumulate an additional $10,000 every year for seven or eight years, when it comes time to buy the new equipment, you might have the capital to do so; you'd at least have assets to borrow against to acquire the equipment.

The key is to have the equipment generate revenues in excess of its depreciation each year.

Financial Power Planning

In producing your financial power plan, your credit rating is one of your most valuable assets. Look for ways to keep it strong. It will pay off over and over again. If you have a strong credit rating, you can get almost anything you want. People who don't know you want to sell you goods, offer you loans, and make deals with you.

When I was president of a conglomerate and someone wanted to check out our credit rating or look at our balance sheet, we were pleased to have them do so. When we negotiated with suppliers we were in an advantageous position. From the outset we frequently received terms that suppliers reserve for their best and longest-standing customers. Often they gave us a better price than the one we proposed.

Any individual can produce their own financial power plan, regardless of how much capital they have to start, simply by

- Looking for ways to build up your bank accounts. Track your average daily balances on your monthly statement.
- Developing a track record for paying your bills promptly.
- Positioning yourself for large purchases using financial or credit information as leverage.

Let's look at some key strategies:

Borrow Money When You Don't Need It to Establish Credit. In my twenties I took out a $100,000 loan that I really did not need and could repay immediately. The reason? By taking out this loan, and quickly repaying, I established a track record and positive credit rating. When I needed funds of more than $100,000, I went back to the bank, they looked up my records and offered me another loan. I established a springboard from which I could quickly acquire a loan when I needed one. I used this method and was able to borrow $1 million before I was thirty years old.

Start That IRA or Roth IRA. If you don't qualify, start one for your children. You can put as little into an IRA as you choose and add to it at your own pace. Remember, you earn nontaxable interest.

Invest in Savings Bonds. When a client or friend of mine has a new baby, I suggest they start a U.S. Savings Bond program in the name of their child. Bonds are purchased at 50 percent of face value, and mature in seven years to ten years (average). Taxes on the interest earned do not have to be paid until the bond is redeemed. Since it's the child's interest, it can be delayed and will usually be at a fairly low rate.

Bonds represent an easy, yet solid, investment plan. I recommend that even my childless clients invest a modest amount in a U.S. Savings Bond plan each year. It's squirreled away money if you need it, and if you don't, you can use their value as asset leverage on your financial statement.

Planning for When the Money Comes

If you are twenty-eight years old and are making $30,000 to $40,000 a year, how are you going to spend your money when you're making $50,000 to $60,000?

What are you going to invest in? Start now to devise a plan for how you are going to manage that greater income. If you've never earned that much and think, *What is the point of trying? I'll make a plan as I approach it,* you are missing an opportunity. Your last-minute plan may create tax liabilities you might have otherwise avoided.

Begin formulating the plan right now, and you'll see what the point is: your personal horizons open up. You begin to consider options that were not in your consciousness before.

You find yourself reading about these potential investments. As you receive more raises and make more money you will already be knowledgeable about preserving your capital. You are more inclined to put the money into investment vehicles that can further accelerate progress toward long-term goals.

Are you planning to get married and have children in a few years? That takes money. Would you like to be earning a passive income: interest, dividends, real estate rentals, and so forth? Do you want to be able to retire at fifty or sixty? Write down the plan now. Estimate the cost of your future plan in terms of income by using the cost of living index for the last twenty years as a projection. Structure your investment plan now and project its growth.

Rule of 72

To figure out how long it will take your money to double, divide 72 by the rate of interest on your savings or investment: Here are some examples:

> 72 divided by 10 percent = 7.2 years
> 72 divided by 8 percent = 9.0 years
> 72 divided by 5 percent = 14.4 years

A Part of the Plan: Befriend Thy Banker. If you seek a home mortgage, the best bank to do business with is the one where you keep your business and savings account. When you negotiate a mortgage and have healthy accounts with the bank, you may be able to reduce the points normally required.

First ask for a mortgage commitment. Once received, request that the loan officer evaluate what you have in her bank—accounts that earn the bank a fair or high return may offset what you might ordinarily be required to pay as points on a mortgage loan. If you run your own business, this tactic will work well for you. Put your excess cash into instruments that pay sensible interest with moderate risk: certificate of deposits, T-bills, or brokerage with the bank from which you will be seeking a mortgage. However, you'll need discipline not to touch the money.

Suppose you are under thirty, don't own a business, and have little or no experience with bankers. Go to an established bank, pick out a loan officer who sounds like someone with whom you can communicate, introduce yourself, and say, "I am here to establish a relationship with this bank. I want to put my savings here, start a checking account, establish trust funds for my children (once I have them), and establish a retirement account, and I want to acquire mortgages."

Today, most banks are equipped to be responsive to this kind of presentation. Later, when you seek and acquire a mortgage commitment, wait a few days and go back to the banker and essentially say, "I have these assets invested in the bank. What will you do for me?" If they can't think of anything, offer suggestions.

All the while you keep building a relationship so that the bank maintains an interest in you and your accounts, and is responsive to your needs. If the bank is not responsive, go to another bank.

For those with a small business (or none at all), I suggest doing business with a major bank at one of their nearby branches. Seek out the manager of the branch with whom you wish to have a banking relationship. Strive to develop a solid interpersonal relationship with the manager. Call the manager regularly. Seek advice, even if you don't need or use it.

When you need help, call the manager. Tell him/her your goals and aspirations. Use EPOD skills in all aspects of communication. If a competitive banker's CD rates go up a quarter of a percent, don't immediately jump to the next bank. Instead, let your banker know when they cease to be competitive. Remain loyal, knowing that a few points in the long run are not as important as the relationship that is building. Let the banker know this.

Make Your Money Work for You. Seek to have several sources of income. It does not make any difference that your salary may not be that large: you can put your money to work for you. Most people's primary source of income is their paycheck, or, if self-employed, the amount of income they can draw from their business.

Secondary sources of income may be derived from home-based businesses, including hobbies that generate income, an investment program, or interest accrued through investment and savings.

Start from wherever you are; make it a part of your plan. Work toward having income from different sources no matter how minuscule it seems at first.

Case #3: No Matter How Little You Earn

My maternal grandfather, Aaron Jacoby, was illiterate, yet he had a greater impact on me than any other man. My grandmother had diabetes, developed glaucoma, and went blind, and in their time they had no hospitalization insurance. Though he only made $40 a week, he bought his house and every other possession with cash. He paid my grandmother's hospital bills, and when he died he left an estate of $14,000. If my estate equals $100 million when I die, I will not have accomplished what that man did. He understood the basic rules of economics, the first of which is to **spend less money than you take in.**

Sounds simple enough, yet here is where discipline plays a major role. I learned from him that if you have a dollar, you spend 80 cents. If you have $10, you spend $8. It doesn't matter what you earn or have, put a piece of it away.

Somehow, some way, you will find room for savings. Practice economic discipline. Delay the frequency of trading in your car. Ask for discounts wherever you are the customer. Don't keep too much money in a demand account that does not pay interest.

Avoid paying interest on credit cards. Use a credit card for convenience and to temporarily delay payments. Once the bill comes, however, try to pay the balance in full. Why pay what amounts to be exorbitant interest (14 to 18 percent and more on some cards)? Unfortunately, most people use their credit cards inappropriately and end up paying dearly for the privilege.

A strong personal power plan includes not paying more interest than you have to.

In business the power plan is to always pay promptly and take advantage of the early payment discount that suppliers offer. In many start-up businesses where there is a cash flow problem, it might be wise to borrow money in order to take advantage of suppliers' discounts. The money you save by making early payments to suppliers would more than offset the cost of the borrowed funds. Do the arithmetic. A $50,000 loan at 8 percent = $4,000 interest for the year. If you discount $50,000 worth of payables at 2 percent, prompt discount earned the first month is $1,000, which equals 25 percent of your total interest payable.

Two percent prompt payment discounts taken regularly earn 37 percent when compounded annually.

Discipline and Planning

What does it take to execute these types of strategies? A power plan and discipline. Devising the plan aids in generating discipline. Executing the plan is a discipline.

Some of what you have earned in the early years can be squirreled away for the later years. This viewpoint is nothing new, but the necessity of having a plan to do this is more important than ever. If you are borrowing up to the hilt, your power plan begins with how you are going to get yourself out of debt. From there your plan details what you will save each month and how much you are going to accumulate by some future point in time.

Some years ago I produced a video entitled *Your Personal Power Plan for Success*, which defines areas in our lives that need addressing. Some important issues included health, nutrition, stress reduction and improving self-esteem. I encourage the reader to check my Web site, www.daveyoho.com, for more information on this informative study.

In the meantime, the following exhibit explains somewhat oversimplistically both the problem and the solution.

THE PROBLEM:

$$\frac{P.M.S. + R.N. + D.E. + A.E.}{D.O.M.S.} = \frac{D/E\ (D)}{P.D.}$$

P.M.S.	=	Poor Management of Stress	D/E	=	Dis-ease
R.N.	=	Reckless Nutrition	(D)	=	Disease
D.E.	=	Disregard for Exercise			
A.E.	=	Adverse Environment			
D.O.M.S.	=	Dependency on Medical Services	P.D.	=	Premature Death

THE PRESCRIPTION:

$$\frac{P.M.S. + R.N. + D.E. + A.E.}{D.O.M.S.} = \frac{F.W.B. + S.W.\ (I)}{E.L.}$$

P.M.S.	=	Proper Management of Stress	F.W.B. + S.W. (I) *		
R.N.	=	Regulated Nutrition	* Feelings of Well Being and Self Worth Increase		
D.E.	=	Disciplined Exercise			
A.E.	=	Affirming Environment			
D.O.M.S.	=	Development of My Self Esteem	E.L.	=	Elongated Life

EPOD Tactics

- **Cash flow:** An interesting method to build cash flow is to place large orders during the last few days of the month, then put them on a corporate credit card. Here is an example.
    - Goods purchased on March 28: $20,000.
    - Paid on credit card on March 28.
    - Shows up as April purchases.
    - Payment due by May 10.
    - If goods are sold in April, you extend your use of money for thirty days.
- Take advantage of prompt discounts when you are able to do so. Otherwise, pay your bills over the longest period of time and collect your money as promptly as possible. This doesn't mean to cheat your suppliers. Pay promptly, then negotiate with them for favorable terms.
- Collections are an important part of any business. They help to improve your cash flow and reduce the need to borrow.
- Just before charging a purchase on your credit card, ask the vendor for a discount if you pay cash immediately. Seek a discount equal to what the vendor pays the credit card company.
- Eliminate products or services that don't pull their weight. If an item represents only 5 to 7 percent of your annual volume, unless there is a strong customer service reason to keep it, get rid of it and concentrate on your other products.
- All entrepreneurs experience their share of disappointing developments. You might believe you're on the right track, and suddenly a shortage in a critical material cripples your business and cash flow. These phenomena, however, are usually temporary; you can always work around them.

CHAPTER 6

Changing the Rules

> "In a time of drastic change, it is the learners who inherit the future. The learned find themselves equipped to live only in a world that no longer exists."
> —Eric Hoffer

What do Robert Redford, Tom Cruise, Paul Newman, Sylvester Stallone, and Dustin Hoffman, as well as movie greats from yesteryear such as Humphrey Bogart, John Garfield, and Kirk Douglas all have in common? They are all below average height (some way below average height), standing less than five-foot-ten. Though we tend to value the tall athletic look, these Hollywood screen actors are among the big screen's great male leads.

What was the driving, underlying force in the lives of these actors to become larger-than-life characters on the screen? I believe they had a deep-seeded need to achieve and to compensate for their shortness of stature. Consciously or subconsciously, it is likely each actor sought what he needed to do to counteract this situation.

Case # 298: The Short Shall Inherit the Slam-Dunk Title

Spud Webb, once an explosive guard for the Atlanta Hawks of the National Basketball Association, was listed at five-foot-eight, but his real height was closer to five-foot-six. He played in a game where tall men reign supreme, yet he won the NBA slam-dunk contest in 1986 over a field of superstars eight to fourteen inches taller than he is. The basket is ten feet high, but to slam-dunk you must be able to reach well over the basket. To dunk, Webb jumped nearly his own height.

The conventional wisdom in basketball was that a five-foot-six player simply could not compete, let alone be a slam-dunk champion. Nevertheless, Webb changed the rules for himself and others, such as five-foot-three Tyrone (Muggsy) Bogues, who made the NBA in 1988. Imagine Bogues in a league where the average player is a foot and a half taller; think of the weight and muscle mass difference.

Most of the average-sized (taller) players told me that Muggsy was always a threat; his arms and hands were so low that if he stole the ball, there was no hope of getting it back, unless he passed it. One player told me playing against Muggsy was the equivalent of trying to keep an enraged pit bull away from your ankles.

Both Webb and Bogues saw their height difference as an advantage. They didn't play by convention; they used blazing speed in their game to drive past taller opponents.

Because they were shorter and closer to the floor, their ball handling was surer. When they hunched over while driving to the basket or passing to a teammate, they forced opposing taller guards to look down at an uncomfortable angle.

Now imagine how it was in high school where the game is structured and positioned for the six-foot-plus athlete. Without high levels of energy (E), optimism (O), and certainly discipline (D), neither of these athletes could have made the NBA.

Winning Our Independence

Over two hundred years ago the rules of warfare were vastly different than they are today. Opposing armies identified themselves with distinctive uniforms. They fought in open fields. On holidays or during inclement weather they abstained from combat. Remember how the American colonists won the Revolutionary War against the British? Behind trees, on Sundays, and in the rain.

Changing the Rules in Business

Assess your competition. Are they large companies? Examine what they are doing. Then find a way to accomplish the same results in a different way or by doing the opposite.

Case # 154: Not Just Another Soap Company

When I was in college, we studied business case histories. The major companies in the soap industry made profits in pennies and often ate their competition. Out of the dozens of industries that started small, most wouldn't go into the soap business. But one company that started small and bucked the trends is now internationally known.

That company was Amway. Their first product? A biodegradable soap which they sold by changing the rules. They sold their soap door-to-door while larger companies like Procter and Gamble continued to sell their products through the supermarket and convenience stores.

Amway sells its product through direct sales. Their product has distinctive labeling and packaging, as well as an advertising story that can be told person to person, all of which represented a major change from the traditional methods of selling soap products. What started as a simple (yet different) kind of soap company became a multi-billion-dollar company.

Other Innovators

In 1880, a book salesman gave small bottles of perfume to homemakers who listened to his sales presentations. When the perfume proved to be more popular than his books, he founded the California Perfume Company, later renamed **Avon** after the English river.

Federal Express Corporation (FedEx) was the inspiration of Fred Smith, who recognized in the late 1960s that the United States was fast becoming a service-oriented economy with a need for reliable overnight delivery service. Smith presented **FedEx's** business concept in a Yale term paper; his grade was a C. The rest is history.

Thomas Monaghan grew up in an orphanage. He developed a strategy of selling pizzas by delivering them hot and fresh within thirty minutes, and locating stores near colleges and military bases. He called his company **Domino's Pizza.**

Joe Albertson left Safeway Corp in 1939 and opened his first food store in Boise, Idaho. The **Albertson** store differed in many ways; among these were: ten thousand square feet of space (approximately eight times the size of his competitors), plenty of free parking, an in-store butcher shop, a bakery, and an ice cream shop. *Voila*: the first supermarket.

The panic of 1873 left Joseph Hudson bankrupt. After he paid his debts at 60 cents on the dollar, he saved enough to open a men's clothing store in Detroit in 1881. Among his innovations were merchandise-return privileges and price marking instead of bargaining. Hudson fully repaid his creditors from 1873—with interest—after **Dayton Hudson** became the largest retailer of men's clothing in America.

In 1941 after a major hailstorm damaged cars in the Washington area, Leo Goodwin founded **GEICO**. He engaged auto shops to work twenty-four hours per day solely for his company. Goodwin's policyholders told friends about the service, and business grew by leaps and bounds.

Food Town, the forerunner of **Food Lion,** was formed in Salisbury, North Carolina, by three former Winn-Dixie employees, Wilson Smith and brothers Ralph and Brown Ketner. Stock was sold at $10 per share to anyone in their hometown who would buy. One of the store's first employees and stockholders was bagger Tom Smith, who became chairman and CEO and retired in 1999. In order to stay in business after the first six months, they decided to cut prices to increase cash flow by 50 percent. The plan worked.

While on vacation in Richmond, Virginia, in 1949, Samuel Wurtzel learned from a local barber that the first TV station in the South was about to go on the air. Wurtzel immediately decided to launch a southern TV retail operation and founded Wards Company, an acronym for family names Wurtzel, Alan, Ruth, David, and Samuel, now known as **Circuit City** Stores.

Case #255: Designer Decks

Dan Betts was a carpenter and designer who ran a small remodeling business. He was intrigued with the number of homeowners who took indoor living outdoors, via a new deck. He also found deck building in large quantities to be complicated: designing it; ordering lumber, fasteners, bolts, nails, screws, and concrete for the footings; then hiring a crew of two or three men with elaborate tools, who could install the deck in three to four days.

So Dan designed and built a factory with a production method similar to the automobile industry. The deck is designed on a computer, then all of its parts and pieces are assembled and transported to a site where it is installed, usually in one day.

Today, his company, **USA Deck,** is the largest of its kind, installing over four thousand decks annually.

Case #138: Becoming "Super" in the Supermarket

When Bob O'Brien was twenty, he was hired for a low-entry job in a supermarket. He didn't have a college education, and the thought of using a computer frightened him. Still, Bob wanted to rise to the management level. So he made himself indispensable.

Bob went to the assistant manager and said, "I've been filling the stock shelves. I know the guy in receiving is overloaded with work. I'd like to help him and learn how the stock comes in." Within a matter of weeks Bob knew two jobs. Next, Bob volunteered to help in purchasing. Before the year ended, Bob had worked in seven departments and was familiar with twenty different jobs. When a new, larger store was opened, Bob applied to work with the start-up team. Before his twenty-third birthday, Bob had become an assistant manager in the large store. When the chain was acquired by a larger company, Bob applied for and received advanced management training, including college courses at the company's expense.

Today Bob manages a division that covers three states.

Case #51: Changing (Not Breaking) the Rules

Change agents frequently operate in uncharted waters with a compass and direction that only they truly understand.

Murray Gross has spent most of his adult life creating change. He was born in Pittsburgh, Pennsylvania, as the country emerged from the Great Depression and would soon face WWII; When he was five, his father left for the U.S. Army, and his parents divorced when he was six. As a result, he moved with his mother and sister to New Martinsville, West Virginia, a rural town of five thousand people, where his grandfather owned a small department store.

Ultimately, he would be adopted by his grandparents and receive his elementary and high school education in an environment where the total student body was four hundred and the high school graduating class was one hundred.

Although his resume does not mention his early training, he learned to sweep and clean his grandfather's store, trim the windows, and even occasionally write the sales slips for those purchasing menswear. At the age of ten he started selling in the store. In a time prior to calculators and adding machines, he developed the skills that rapidly enabled him to add long columns of figures. Those who meet with him today marvel at his ability to do complicated arithmetic in his head.

Frequently, he went to breakfast meetings with his grandfather, who met with the town's other retailers. While there he absorbed the jargon and pros and cons of business, along with an understanding of what made customers satisfied.

Graduating as a straight-A student, he was valedictorian of his graduating class. He then went to the University of Pittsburgh with the intention of studying pre-law. However, the fates intervened. His grandfather passed away. He returned to New Martinsville to help his grandmother and didn't get the opportunity to complete his last year of college. Perhaps all the early changes in his life led him to develop his style for interacting with change, calamity, and paradigm shifts.

At the age of twenty-two, already married, he took an interim job with a construction company and ultimately moved into their kitchen design program. Unknowingly, this career move would ultimately affect the majority of his future business endeavors. He was mentored in his sales skills by an older, highly skilled salesperson. Within three years every facet of the business became familiar to him. At about that time he noticed that a local lumber yard chain named Busy Beaver was growing rapidly, and he proposed to their management that he and his sales mentor set up a kitchen division within the lumber yard which would offer a brand-new concept in that market. Their slogan was: "Do it yourself, or we'll do it for you."

He designed and implemented the means by which the products and services were advertised, displayed, demonstrated, sold, financed, and installed—a radical undertaking for a brash entrepreneur barely past his teens. In a space of fifteen years the business grew to a $12 million company at a time when a successful competitor would have been congratulated for doing $1 million annually. By today's standards that $12 million would equal $50 million to $60 million. His rapidly expanding company came to the attention of a major (Fortune 500) public corporation that, while being impressed with the growth and the ingenuity of the marketing program and the extraordinary customer satisfaction level, was even more impressed with the company's methods for recruiting, training, and compensating salespeople. Murray Gross had received national attention from the building and remodeling industry, and shortly thereafter the company—Cyclops Steel—acquired Busy Beaver.

Now Murray moved on to his next challenge. A successful New York manufacturer had developed a system for manufacturing kitchen cabinet facing, which was sold through a licensed dealer organization. The concept was to fabricate for homeowners new countertops, doors, and drawer facings. Once manufactured, replacing an existing kitchen took less than two days. In the late 1980s, this idea was being promoted to compete with kitchen remodeling, which might take six to ten weeks while grossly inconveniencing the homeowners. The successful manufacturer had a comfortable, moderate-sized business doing between $1 million and $2 million annually. In 1987, Murray Gross brought his marketing and sales know-how to Facelifter Home Systems, and by 1995 the company was doing $50 million with 24 branches and 120 salespeople, and had become the largest cabinet facing company in the United States. In 1991 they became a public corporation and were once again acquired by another public corporation. The shareholders received $78 million.

Murray Gross, through his unique methods, had built a cadre of exceptional marketers and salespeople. Those who followed him through the journey to that point say that he built the business on three factors: sincerity, trust, and finding ways to have others believe in you.

Finally, the change agent and risk taker embarked on his greatest coup. In 1997 with eight investors, he bought the assets of a then-bankrupt company, a $2.5 million investment—again, a company that manufactured and sold cabinet facing. Starting from ground zero, in one year he built a $16 million company and today as a public corporation his company is projected to do over $120 million in revenue. It has its own finance company and owns the largest deck manufacturing and installation company in the United States.

The company, U.S. Home Systems, of which Murray Gross is C.E.O. and chairman, is also a marketing arm for Home Depot and Century 21.

Murray Gross has made it possible for many of his loyal employees who had stock options to earn amounts of money that might otherwise be considered impossible. He believes that the key to becoming a change agent involves remembering the lessons he learned from his grandparents, Albert and Sarah, in their small store in New Martinsville, West Virginia. By using his love of study and education, he continues to expand his knowledge of businesses and the people who are necessary to run them.

Murray Gross wears his optimism like an illuminated sign. He is a smiling affirmer of others, who mentors the executives of his company as he does his family. He constantly examines means and methods for those in his company to grow.

He has developed extraordinary skills as a negotiator, all based on his concept of creating winning situations for both sides. He believes persuasion is largely a matter of helping others get what they want.

Running a public corporation requires, above all else, discipline. The actions of the board of directors and the audit committee will always be subject to scrutiny. In the case of Murray Gross, however, the credos learned from his storekeeper grandfather are the foundation of his discipline.

"Be sure to share, and look at issues through the other person's eyes, and you will have the confidence to do the right thing."

Everyone Can Change the Rules

Whatever impediments and obstacles you had early in life, it's likely that they are still present in some form. Each of us has the capability to reflect on our life's experiences, learn from them, and apply them in positive ways. It is a proven fact that many individuals compensate for their impediment, deficiency, or lack by training, compensating, or even overcompensating.

Winston Churchill became a great speaker despite his early years as a stutterer. Mel Tillis also overcame his stuttering to become a country/western singer. Nelson Rockefeller as governor, vice president, and political leader made hundreds of speeches, and few knew he was dyslexic.

A young high school athlete named Dick Fosbury had difficulty mastering the scissor kick system of high jumping. So he practiced a rule-changing method. He ran to the bar and at the appropriate moment he turned his back to the bar and literally threw his body over in the backward position. Onlookers either laughed or were stunned. As he worked his way into track meets competing coaches protested his unorthodox method. However, no rules were broken; they were just changed. Today his method is used by a large majority of high jump competitors and is called the Fosbury Flop.

As a child, because of a congenital defect, I was required to undergo speech therapy in the school system. I hated it. I often felt like the lowest form of human being. I was forced to do speech exercises and even speak in front of my class. At times it seemed hopeless to try, and the harder I tried, the more hopeless the situation seemed. However, after some years of training, I developed a technique that made my impediments almost undetectable. I also learned very early the practices of enunciation, projection, and resonance. When I am complimented today on my deep voice, I frequently acknowledge how my speech therapy led me to techniques that escalated my career, where I have been paid to make thousands of speeches.

I realize I received early training in a skill that the typical adult would prefer to avoid: speaking to others, particularly public speaking. The impediment and the lessons I hated slowly became my forte. My weakness became my strength.

Case #464: Let There Be Juice

At the age of fifty-one Bob Olson embarked on a new job representing a company providing services to laboratories that needed technical assistance. Though untrained in any technology, he was a good listener, a keen observer, and a critical thinker.

During the early 1970s, while in a food products company laboratory, a purchasing agent lamented the overpurchase of two truckloads of apple juice concentrate. Bob asked and was told that each truck contained seventy-two drums (fifty-five gallons each). The value of each truckload was in excess of $50,000. He asked for and was given permission to sell the overpurchase, and, if he sold, he would earn a commission for his efforts.

He sat down with a phone book and called any company who he believed might be interested in buying apple juice concentrate. Next day, on a personal visit to a major food chain's headquarters, he sold both truckloads and earned a commission of $2,200.

Bob immediately became Robert H. Olson, Juice Concentrate Broker. Business cards, order forms, and a new phone number certified he was in business, notwithstanding the fact that those in that industry are usually chemists with special training in food technology. They also know the industry and the industry knows them.

Undaunted, Bob called on every company who might buy or have a future interest in juice concentrate. He circulated letters and called growers all over the world. He joined the Institute of Food Technology and attended every meeting. He also volunteered to be the official greeter at each function, thus assuring that he met every attendee in person, exchanged business cards and became known on a first-name basis.

Within five years, operating out of a small office with his wife Norma, his only employee, he built the largest juice concentrate brokerage firm in the United States.

Each week, on Thursday, a card was mailed to each customer, to be received on Monday, the big order day. The card contained a quote, an inspiring thought, or an "Olson chuckle," as he called them.

Long before the computer made ordering and transferring information a mechanical and impersonal chore, Bob used constant personal contact and follow-up to build customer relationships. His customers were giant companies like Coca-Cola, who purchased in truckloads and tank cars, and small accounts buying five drums a month. Irrespective of size or status, everyone got Olson's personal attention.

Growers from all over the world asked him to sell their products. His pineapple concentrate came from Taiwan. Other products came from countries throughout the world, as well as the United States.

In recognition of his many accomplishments, the prestigious Institute of Food Technology named one of their highest awards the "Robert H. Olson Award."

Bob Olson is quick to point out that beyond his creative start, there was a business plan and policy, the basis of which was: be selective in the suppliers, maintain tight shipping schedules (particularly with refrigerated tank cars), treat all incoming calls with high energy, and keep an optimistic outlook on life and share that feeling with everyone you meet.

There is certainly more to every story than what appears in the synopsis. There is often unrewarded effort, setbacks, disappointments, and a frequent desire to toss in the towel. Here is where optimism and discipline are necessary to complement the high-energy, persuasive tactics of the ultimate rule-changing achiever.

Case #235: Changing the Rules with High Energy

Many people regard their work as mundane. Suppose you had to explain to a group of salespeople how a credit statement is prepared and used. They probably wouldn't respond with much energy, and, as previously explained, your energy could decrease. Instead of writing a long manual on how to use a credit statement, Sheila Parker, a marketing assistant for a large company, produced a snazzy illustration that highlighted the six major points she wanted to make. Then she explained her chart with high energy, using analogies, humor, even short skits.

Parker realized that most salespeople don't read instructions and complicated, technical diagrams. She appealed to their right brain by adding high energy in presenting left-brain-type information.

Because she changed the rules and displayed creativity and zest where it was unexpected, people began to respond to her presentation.

She was then put in charge of all in-house presentations. Today she heads the training department of her company and makes many presentations at association meetings.

Case #20: The Overcrowded Classroom

Show me a good professor, and I'll guarantee he or she brings energy, persuasion, and enthusiasm into the environment. When students say they like to take a professor's class, what are they really saying? The professor is unique and upbeat and stimulates their intellect.

Many years ago, I entered the auditorium at the University of Cincinnati to observe the late Professor William (Bill) McGrane's class, "Orientation to Business," and I was about to be oriented. More than one thousand students were in attendance, and space limitation had prevented others from signing up.

Music played from large speakers, then faded as the class began, and Professor McGrane took center stage. Holding a dozen jumping ropes in his hand he said, "Who wants one?" and eager volunteers ran up to grab the ropes and participate in the first exercise. With a musical background, twelve students jumped to the beat while the others in the audience clapped in unison. Within five minutes this upbeat audience was ready for the lecture series on "How to Market Yourself in Search of a Job."

In an environment where learning is seen as a task, cramming for tests is exhausting, and contemplating one's future employment is frightening, the late Bill McGrane changed the rules, making learning exciting and educationally enjoyable.

When you bring high energy to a situation where people are not expecting it, you are changing the rules in your favor.

McGrane's main thrust in life was education. As a former superintendent of schools, he found that people of all ages and occupations learned at a more rapid pace when they were encouraged to be creative, enthusiastic, and even provocative. Once a month he held his sessions on building sound self-esteem for the leaders of corporate America. Although now deceased, McGrane's concepts have enriched the lives of the many he taught and mentored. His "changing the rules" curriculum still endures.

Optimism and Changing the Rules

When you review all those things in your life that haven't worked, think again. What difficult childhood or teenage lesson did you learn that has utility today?

Like the child who at age twelve hated piano lessons and at forty-two now loves to play the piano, what did you endure that has become a strength, a blessing, a special ability, or an optimistic development?

With a little tolerance and determination the obstacles you face can be your strengths. An optimistic outlook? You bet. A realistic outlook? Most assuredly. It has been said that "man has built most nobly when limitations were greatest." Maybe you can't convert every impediment into a strength, but in an optimistic light consider how you can change the rules in your favor.

Suppose you operate a small market and your competitor has fourteen stores. His strength may be his proximity to customers in various neighborhoods. How could you meet this challenge? Advertise around town: "If you live within walking distance to those other stores, I will deliver for you," "I will pick you up and bring you back." Turn the competitor's advantage into your advantage.

Case #310: Fourth in Line for Promotion

Larraine Colter was fourth in line for the job she wanted; those ahead of her were all capable, and she felt as if the situation was stacked against her. So she listed all of her pluses: character traits, strengths, experiences, and relationships, and she picked the area where she felt she was the strongest: stamina.

Then she considered other aspects of the job and the work environment. Among the people proceeding up the ladder one had an MBA; she did not. She decided to work in the office an extra hour beyond what the MBA worked. Later, when the MBA got the job Colter wanted, she successfully pursued another job, becoming the MBA's assistant. Today she heads the department and supervises the activities of thirty-seven people (three of whom have MBAs).

Discipline and Changing the Rules

How well do you handle the things that (at least initially) you don't like to do? A fundamental career discipline is that if your career is to continue to grow, you cannot coast. Devote a certain amount of time each day or week to professional reading to ensure that you understand new situations and trends. Constantly develop your listening skills. It's an area where most people think that they are proficient but are really lacking.

Continually go to seminars; the world is changing too fast to do otherwise.

Most people agree that they need to study and grow, but they quickly equivocate by saying, "I don't have time to stay on top of everything."

If you don't have the time, then you lack the discipline. Change the rules to keep pace. Consider something that you would like to accomplish. Before saying you don't have the time, examine what you are doing now. Can anything be done simultaneously? What can you let slide or drop? If you commute thirty minutes to work, and your goal is to learn a foreign language, buy a cassette or CD to use during this time. You'll give five hours a week to this goal, and in a short time you will develop this language skill.

Discipline in Reading. If your goal is to read a three-hundred-page book with only ten minutes each night before sleep, set a goal to read three to five pages nightly.

If you want to read a book to further your career or development, change the rules: instead of reading from front to back, go to the index or pick some key areas, and read those first. Then move forward and back throughout the book. If you're bored right now, go to the index of this book. Find something that appeals to you, and devote a few minutes to reading that section.

Within families, a great way to complete a book is to read alternate chapters aloud. A husband and wife, father and son, or two siblings could read alternate chapters and then present the other person with an opinion on the segments covered. This brings families closer, breaks up monotony, and provides a fuller understanding of the material.

Managing Your Investments. Use discipline and change the rules to manage your investments. I have a complex investment program, and I can't monitor each investment daily. So I changed the rules by finding brokers who are able to follow my precise instructions. To simplify my understanding, I maintain a chart of my investments on computer and update it periodically. I use the chart to see when I bought a stock, its low and high, and the last date I checked it.

What charts and graphs can you devise to monitor what otherwise seems cumbersome and time consuming? Calories consumed? Workouts? Sales progress? Constructing a chart is a discipline.

After a while you may need to revise it—more discipline.

> With creativity and ingenuity you can structure your surroundings to support you.

If you believe you're stuck in your office all day, particularly if you eat lunch there and are exposed to idle chatter, use a headset and listen to your favorite album a few days out of every week. It's enough of a change to help you maintain a healthy balance.

If you dislike standing in a bank line, then bank by mail or have someone else stand in line.

Within our schedules, our to-do lists—the things that we tend to regard as fixed and unchangeable—are actually quite changeable.

Case #6: Dawn Gray Blend

One of the companies I ran during my career was a multi-state roofing business with twenty-two branch offices. Although there were many colors available for the shingles on the roof, lighter colors were becoming popular because they reflected ultraviolet rays. With twenty-two branch offices I was concerned about inventory; it was costly to stock twenty colors in each location.

I devised a system where one color accounted for 90 percent of our sales. This proved to be a very profitable product that was a practical choice and looked great on homes.

Dawn gray blend included speckles of green, yellow, browns, and red, and yielded several benefits to the purchaser. First, the blend made it difficult to detect defects, dirt, or anything that landed on the roof. Second, if a consumer was having trouble choosing a color, the blend matched many different colors and styles and became a quick and effective choice.

The key to having it work in the business was training the salespeople. As our sales staff became more effective at selling it, the dawn gray blend often became the only color that they had to show to prospects. We trained our people to say, "When looking at your house, I think this is the best color." Most people simply did not have a preference.

Eventually the company I ran became the largest residential roofing company in the United States. The cost-effective one-color program saved customers money because we could buy in great quantities, which added to our profitability. My business could not have grown at the same pace if I had to maintain substantial roofing inventories.

The key to effectively changing the rules is to do it in a manner in which you benefit other people, not hurt them.

EPOD Tactics

- To improve cash flow and expand more rapidly, the Marriott Corporation designs, builds, and opens hotels, then syndicates and sells them while maintaining their name on the structure and the right to manage it. They don't own the bricks and mortar, yet they control their use.
- Encourage customers, associates, and friends to use your email address. Respond with one, two or three sentences.
- Speed read your correspondence and use a highlighter. Jot your response directly on the letter, make a copy, and return the letter. It is quick, it is good business, and we find most respondents appreciate the prompt response and are not offended.
- Change your voice mail. They are all starting to sound the same. Visit my Web site, www.daveyoho.com, for free information: Voice Mail, Friend or Foe.
- Instead of turning on the news each morning and hearing the details of rapes, murders, or fires, play fifteen minutes of a stimulating cassette or CD. Play another fifteen minutes on your way to work, on your way home, and before you go to sleep at night. Thirty or forty minutes of listening daily is the equivalent of reading one-third of a book, and if you like what you hear, repeat it often.
- Make a list of those things you do daily. Then review the list. See which activities could be merged, reassigned, reduced, or eliminated.
- Life is the process of continuing growth. With continuing growth comes some pain; you have to be ready for some setbacks at any stage of your life.

- Meet with and interview unusual, unique people. Determine in advance that you will learn something new each day.
- Visit the library in person or browse new information on the Internet. Read about something you've never heard of before.
- Pick a page at random in a dictionary or encyclopedia, and learn a new word or phrase.

CHAPTER 7

Selling and EPOD Solutions

"Whenever an interaction between two or more parties takes place, for the purpose of establishing new ideas, exchanging goods or services, or the development of a relationship, some form of selling will occur and the skills of the communicator will determine the outcome."
—Dave Yoho, "Everybody Sells"

Many people are deluded or simply misunderstand the selling process, frequently assessing it as manipulation, chicanery, or worse. Webster's Third New International Dictionary contains over fifty definitions, some as simple as "exchange property, goods or service for money" or "to establish faith, confidence or belief in." Then, within the same group of definitions are phrases such as "a trick or hoax" and "to cheat or dupe."

In fact, it isn't the numerous definitions that cause the confusion, rather the various ways in which we humans devise methods of communication in an effort to convince others, change mind-sets, or promote the sale of goods and services.

Having observed the "persuasive communication" scene for over fifty years while noticing the subtle, yet dynamic change in selling methods as well as buying modalities, I have reached conclusions that are embodied in six Power Statements.

I urge you as a reader not to jump to any rapid conclusions before I define each, and to keep in mind a catchphrase that I have used for thirty years: "The Power of an Idea Can Be Measured by the Degree of Resistance It Attracts."

Here are the Power Statements:

POWER STATEMENT #1: Most people do not like to sell.

POWER STATEMENT #2: Most people do not know how to sell.

POWER STATEMENT #3: As a product or service increases in popularity and use, traditionally the skills of those selling it diminish.

POWER STATEMENT #4: Selling is the least understood function within most companies.

POWER STATEMENT #5: Despite varying degrees of marketing success, many companies are inept in teaching or training salespeople to get the order (close the sale).

POWER STATEMENT #6: Whenever an interaction between two or more parties takes place for the purpose of establishing new ideas, exchanging goods or services, or the development of a relationship, some form of selling will occur and the skills of the communicator will determine the outcome.

Our examination of each of these statements is colored by the many and varied situations in which selling skills are seemingly a necessity.

In retailing, the environment created by the retailer can make the customer comfortable. Purchases are made after the customer rapidly perceives that the store is reputable, the merchandise is sound, and the sales help is credible. Contemporary thinking seems to indicate that extensive selling skills are not that important when the environment is conducive to doing business.

If the latter is true, what has occurred when a potential customer enters a retail establishment with a purchase in mind, only to leave annoyed, frustrated, or disillusioned and without making a purchase? In short, a malfunction in the process has taken place, which in turn caused the methodology to fail.

In industrial selling the salesperson is often trying to establish, maintain, or upgrade an account and may be competing with an existing vendor. Here, the wisdom indicates selling will require prospecting, follow through, dogged determination, repetitive calls, special deals, and sometimes flamboyant ingenuity.

The complexity of this latter structure is that it frequently calls for the salesperson to react with a response pattern that is contrary to his or her behavior or inconsistent with one's personality.

Prevailing wisdom born out of extensive research defines personality as "an individual's enduring persistent response patterns across a variety of situations." Further, these response patterns are developed based on the individual's history, beliefs, attitude, motivational drive, and other complicated issues. Thus, much of what passes for training in industrial selling isn't that effective.

The upside of this extensive research is the validation that human beings are inherently adaptive, if supplied with methodology that enables them to cope with ever-changing patterns of society.

In any case, where the skill level of the salespeople has been raised by creating a strong sales methodology augmented by training and supervision, the outcome usually results in increased volume and profitability.

Many organizations that achieve dominant market share tend to relax their training or give little value to upgrading the skills of their salespeople. As a result, despite their apparent success, volume profitability and customer satisfaction often decline.

In a rapidly growing business, marginal selling skills may not impede a company's overall growth. When there is a malfunction or drastic change in the economy or marketplace, such as increased competition or declining demand, the salesperson frequently lacks the skills necessary to be more competitive, retain current accounts, or build a new customer base. What is called "selling" often is not.

Corporate America seems to be searching for an overly intellectualized concept of sales success and/or to ultimately remove the face-to-face selling that created markets in the first place. Almost 80 percent of modern sales training seems to consist of instilling the basics on a repetitive and reinforcing basis.

Most salespeople require simple, basic instruction, which includes structured sales presentations and presentation books. After mastering the basics, salespeople can be encouraged to master more sophisticated processes of interpersonal relations between buyer and seller. Unfortunately, despite what companies believe to be efficient training, it is not uncommon that about one-fifth of a sales organization produces 50 percent or more of a company's total sales volume. Another fifth of the salespeople are constantly battling personal problems, such as divorces, legal problems, chemical dependency; some are lazy, and many are simply mis-hires.

The balance represents 60 percent of the sales organization. The question is, "Can they be stimulated to upgrade their individual skills and thereby add to increased volume and profitability?"

We observe that the most successful sales groups have a system that stimulates growth in the top and middle echelons, and a plan to replace those mis-hires while at the same time improving their selection process.

Power Statement #1:
Most People Do Not Like to Sell

At seminars this statement attracts flak like a magnet held over iron filings. Salespeople and their managers frequently protest; they evoke their love of selling the products they represent. Then I ask pointed questions and request that participants raise their hands.

For example, I ask, Have you ever . . .

- Had an appointment where the prospect was one or more hours late?

- Had a prospect who didn't show at all?
- Been allotted half the time you anticipated to make your presentation?
- Been promised an order and didn't get it?
- Lost an order you were sure of to lower prices?
- Gotten an order that was turned down by your credit department?
- Had a large order cancelled?
- Had a customer get upset because of late or incomplete delivery, and take it out on you?
- Made a prospecting call in temperatures over 95 or under 30 degrees, or when it is raining or snowing?

Then I ask, How many like or enjoy any of these tasks or circumstances?

None of these occurrences are fun, yet they constitute a major portion of sales activity. Why would salespeople enjoy that part of the role? For the most part, they don't.

Getting an order, receiving kudos for performance, getting paid a sizeable commission, or winning a sales contest are the enjoyable parts of selling, yet they represent a relatively small part of a salesperson's time and activity. Once a manager recognizes the indisputable truth that most people do not like to sell, there is a greater possibility of dealing openly and more effectively with the sales personnel.

The most disciplined salespeople achieve the greatest earnings because they recognize that calling on prospects, staying organized, traveling long distances, having appointments or orders cancelled, facing the possibility of rejection, and overcoming objections are simply steps in the process that leads to sale success.

Superstar salespeople have found a way to deal with issues such as these and even use many of them to their advantage. However, superstars probably represent less than 1 percent of all salespeople.

Over the years I have had the great fortune to meet and work with many sales superstars. Some, like Jack Studnicky, were tall and good-looking and brought new meaning to the word "persuasive"; some, like Jack Fiore, were short in stature and did not have a commanding voice or presence, yet outsold almost everyone in their industry. Pam Richardson, one of a few women in a sales organization of over one thousand, was the top salesperson five years in succession. Her vice president of sales presented her with a Rolex watch so many times, he joked that she had a part-time business running a jewelry store.

In every case these superstars and hundreds of others whom I have met found a way to deal with those unpleasantries I mentioned earlier by what we call "the law of compensating devices"—in short, taking the unpleasant part of the task and developing a methodology that enables them to excel in that area. Alas, if only more companies could recognize this and work on programs that teach others its importance.

Case #77: An EPOD Super Salesperson

My mother used to say, "Big things often come in small packages," and my father used to reply quickly, "So does poison." The truth is many superstars are uniquely packaged and are frequently not perceived as such immediately.

Many years ago, I hired an unlikely superstar as a salesperson. He was intelligent and had a great education. He had a military background and a fine family. However, he had no experience and few skills that would recommend him for a sales role.

After three intense interviews weeks apart, I hired George M. Neall as a trainee salesperson, purely on feelings rather than provable data. It turned out to be one of the smartest hires I ever made.

He exhibited an energy level unlike any salesperson I ever hired. He worked twelve-hour days while other salesmen worked eight or nine. He did this, he said, to compensate for his lack of experience and sales know-how.

He was easily trained. He followed the dictates of our sales system, and because he tended to be left-brained he took notes on everything. He spent whatever hours he had left and Sundays (he chose to work six days a week) to review and practice to develop the skills to be a productive, successful salesperson.

Prior to starting my own business, I worked for a large company with seventy-two branches and five hundred salespeople. By the end of his first year, George was the seventh-best volume producer in the company, and in his second year he became number three. In the early stages his lack of selling skills was buoyed by his unbelievable energy and overwhelming optimism. He had a driving determination about everything he did and the discipline to make sure he did it correctly.

Over the years, I was fortunate to have employed many super salespeople. On a scale of 1 (low) to 10 (high) some of them were 11 or 12. However, George always stood out as the most consistent, dependable, and thorough salesperson I ever had the good fortune to hire. His ability to deal with all kinds and styles of customers coupled with his insatiable desire to increase his skills paid off handsomely. While he lacked some skills, he made up for it by working harder and longer than his contemporaries.

In the behavioral sciences we refer to this as the law of compensating devices. Although the concept is easy to understand, most of the time getting those with lesser skills in certain areas of life to utilize their talents is difficult. George Neall never studied psychology or sociology, yet unquestionably he was an example of compensating balances.

We became friends, and our careers moved forward together. When I became the president of a conglomerate, he became the treasurer and then, despite his sales skills, his left-brain dominance kicked in. He made the major engineering and purchasing decisions in our company. He sat on the board and reviewed in detail every decision we made that affected operational or financial positioning. He was our safety valve. When everyone wanted to move forward rapidly on a marketing idea, George was the one who urged caution and often withheld his vote pending further due diligence. Issues of investing, finance, and real estate were also his bailiwick, and his energy and disciplines were often at odds with my marketing and sales executives who wanted to make rapid decisions and move on.

Because of George Neall, our company remained financially sound. He always undertook extra due diligence before we acquired other companies, and he did it all in a quiet way that drew no attention to himself.

Executives who joined our company at a later time and were not aware of his original role as a salesperson were often shocked at his balance of skills. As the years grew I began to better understand George as someone who brought energy, persuasion, optimism, and discipline to every aspect of his business and personal life. He was unquestionably a role model for those who sought fully balanced career development.

When our conglomerate was sold, he moved on to land development, high finance, and landfill management; none of those who knew him well were the least surprised at the constant extension of his skills and his ongoing success in diverse endeavors.

My wish for my clients is that they also hire an EPOD superstar someday. Yet, I wonder: will they know it when they meet him or her?

Power Statement #2: Most People Do Not Know How to Sell

This statement also tends to upset those who consider themselves professional salespeople. In truth, it is possible to have varying levels of success in selling without recognizing that which you do not know. However, suppose salespeople were exposed to new techniques and information which enabled them to increase their productivity without a giant effort; the salesperson, the company, and the customer would all benefit from this.

The late Dr. Marvin Jolson, who was at one time senior vice president of Encyclopedia Britannica and later professor emeritus at the University of Maryland, stated:

Historically, the goal of the sales call could be described as an isolated encounter that hopefully resulted in a conquest or victory called a "sale." In the new millennium, the concept is described as a problem-solving discussion between salesperson and prospect that leads toward a meeting of minds that deepens the dependence of each on the other. The salesperson's primary aim should be to collaborate effectively and establish mutual trust.

When related to a sound sales methodology that statement might convert to: "The prospect/customer is the key ingredient in a sound sales methodology. How the prospect thinks and feels has to be the major consideration in the development of a sales system—or that system will eventually fail."

When the issue of customer feelings or values is raised, many managers get uncomfortable, assuming that we're moving into areas often called touchy-feely—yet these same managers want their salespeople to build trust and create rapport in their customer relationships.

Rapport is a state of mind that begins with kinesthetics (feelings). To some salespeople building rapport seems a snap while others try and never seem to get it.

Rapport is most easily developed in the early stages of contact. It is usually based on understanding how prospects think and feel and can be explained this way. Prospects

- Like people who listen to them.
- Like people who endorse their values.
- Like people who work at uncovering their needs.

Those few statements are pretty simple. So then, why is it most salespeople start, then infuse their presentations, with first-person statements such as: I, we, me, my company, my product, and so on?

Next, they interrupt, end sentences, and draw absolute conclusions from simple statements made by prospects.

As an aftermath of a sales contact, a prospect is often labeled as "a price buyer," "tough negotiator," "difficult to deal with," "a shopper," or "just curious." In truth, the salesperson might well be labeled "poorly trained."

A seventeen-year study by my company of the science and practice of successful communication, entitled **Power Linguistics**, provided me with great insights as to why certain sales practices were so successful while others were mediocre or ineffective.

Our study uncovered companies that taught selling methods akin to "get the order at almost any cost." There were also companies who believed that buying should supersede selling, thus allowing almost no modern selling techniques.

The latter believed that injecting questioning techniques, following prescribed presentation methods, or even asking for the order violated some ethical/decency code that presumably offended customers. The former often used archaic selling methods that built little or no customer satisfaction.

When our study took us to interview thousands of customers we were able to discern what the thinking and feeling was of those who had interacted with salespeople. The revealing information enabled us to structure an objective overview of face-to-face selling. We found that prospects most frequently purchase products/services based on the following perceptions:

- Credibility of salesperson
- Rapport with salesperson
- Consideration of their (the prospect's) value system
- Unique quality product/service tailored to their needs
- A product/service that was superior to most other options
- A value that equaled or exceeded the price
- Ease, simplicity of purchase
- The seller was a knowledgeable specialist

As an outgrowth of this study we draw the following supportive conclusions:

- There is no such thing as a cold, rational, dispassionate buyer who buys solely on merit. Most decisions to buy are

based on emotion. Therefore, purely logical arguments and statistical presentations alone are largely ineffective.
- Buyers are usually prompted and motivated by a number of emotional prods, all of which are based on the salesperson's application of a sound sales methodology.

Power Linguistic Sales Training embodies the concept of convincing prospects or customers that they need or desire the product or idea you want them to buy. The use of selected words and phrases enables salespeople to create want that did not exist before.

The proper use of a sound sales methodology is an individual accomplishment. Some salespeople respond to Power Linguistic Training more rapidly than others, and much depends on the trainer.

Power Linguistic Sales Training involves thinking in advance about why a salesperson is going to call on a certain prospect or customer and what will appeal most to their buying motives. Every prospect is different. Therefore, a decision is needed regarding which approach will appeal most to each customer or prospect in a particular circumstance or situation.

The salesperson is still the total technician. Her or his responsibility is to respond to the sales methodology by interpreting its various levels to the prospect/buyer. The salesperson's job and duty are to bring to the surface subliminal desires and to interpret the product or service in terms of the prospect's/buyer's needs. The responsibility of the salesperson is to convince the prospect that the product (service) is best because it meets the prospect's needs better than any competitor's product/service.

Numerous differences between industrial and consumer selling (buying) create variances in presentation and selling styles. However, once the awareness of a need is triggered into a want, the prospect/buyer reverts to the status of a human being; therefore, while the components of the sales methodology may vary, the elements of communication and the need for methodology do not.

Armed with this information, you, the reader, will have a clearer understanding of Power Statements 3 and 4 (which, to refresh your memory, are repeated here):

POWER STATEMENT #3: As a product or service increases in popularity and use, traditionally the skills of those selling it diminish.

POWER STATEMENT #4: Selling is the least understood function within most companies.

Not to Pick On the U.S. Auto Industry, but . . .

I have represented many companies within the automotive industry. I enjoy the people in the industry, my earnings, and the challenges that I face. The automobile industry, however, employs many antiquated techniques when it comes to selling. Today, the vast majority of automobile sales representatives still see each customer as a one-shot deal. But the young man or woman who walks into the showroom is going to buy eight to ten cars over the next twenty to thirty years and may represent an average of $200,000 to $400,000 or more in purchases, including new autos, parts, and services.

Case #11: Working in "the Zone"

My wife and I were shopping for a new Audi. On a Friday evening, about three miles from our home, we visited a dealership that displayed Audis, Porsches, and Mercedes. The showroom was a large, lavish, multimillion-dollar structure with an art gallery on one of its levels. The cars were all polished to a high luster and beautifully displayed.

We spent about twenty minutes looking at the various cars displayed, but no sales representative approached us. We decided to find help. I saw a man leaning on the balcony above the display area. I indicated that if he was an employee, I would like to speak to him. He motioned for me to come upstairs. So I did. Here is our conversation:

Sales Manager:	What can I do for you?
Me:	Do you work here?
Sales Manager:	I'm the sales manager here (no name offered).
Me:	Great, because I'm looking to buy a car.
Sales Manager:	Well, that's the business we're in.
Me:	I wasn't sure.
Sales Manager:	Why . . . what . . . I don't understand.
Me:	My wife and I have been looking at your cars for about twenty minutes, and no salespeople approached us.
Sales Manager:	I see.
Me:	There seem to be quite a few people in those little office cubicles downstairs.
Sales Manager:	Yes, those are our salespeople.
Me:	I'm wondering why none of them came over to speak to us.
Sales Manager:	Well, what kind of car were you looking for?
Me:	An Audi.
Sales Manager:	That's easy to explain. Most of those salespeople are Porsche and Mercedes salespeople.
Me:	Great. Now tell me, how did they know what kind of car I was looking for?

He assured me that they were interested in our business. He asked us to stand near the Audi in the center of the showroom and he would send a salesperson to help. Minutes later, we were approached by a neat, well-dressed young man.

He introduced himself, apologized for our inconvenience, and then uttered the four most unproductive words in retailing: "May I help you?" From that point, it was downhill as far as his sales skills were concerned. Immediately, he waxed enthusiastically to me about Audi's great mileage, its comfort for someone who spent a lot of time commuting, and how it had all the features of larger so-called luxury cars. He was only slightly abashed when told that the car was for my wife.

Without a break in his speech, he then directed his attention to selling my wife this car. He never asked what she was presently driving (an Audi). He did not seek to know if she had driven this model before (she had). In fact, she had owned two Audis previously and had shopped for and driven this very model elsewhere. Can you feel the information opportunities missed?

The salesman opened the hood and elaborated on the overhead cam engine. I was impressed. He commented on the superiority of the braking system, and how the Germans had that department down pat, far ahead of American manufacturers.

Finally, he invited us to his office cubicle. For the next ten minutes he discussed how their dealership was number two in Audi sales on the East Coast, and how he knew this was the best dealer because he originally worked in the zone. (For a moment, I thought he meant the Twilight Zone.) After I suggested it he had our car appraised, then told us the cost of a new Audi with ours as a trade-in. He told us we could probably get an Audi for less elsewhere but not from such a great dealer; they didn't have to give large discounts because they were number two in sales.

We thanked him for his time. I gave him my business card, which was only fair because he had given me his. The next day, we bought an Audi at the same price from a dealer eighteen miles from our home. During the entire interaction the first salesman had never asked our names, nor had he asked

- Whom the car was for?
- Had we ever owned or driven an Audi?
- How long we had owned our Audi?
- What we liked about our last Audi?
- What we would like in a new one?
- Our familiarity with the new model?
- How many miles the car would be driven annually?

- Would it be used for business?
- The number of children in our family?

Why didn't he ask us any of the above questions? The answer, in all probability, is as follows:

- He didn't think of it.
- He hadn't been trained.
- Worse, he didn't care.

How well did this manager and salesman interact with my wife and I based on the EPOD theory? Although the salesman was somewhat enthusiastic, the energy conveyed to us was moderate. The persuasiveness was almost nonexistent. There was some optimism—they had pride in their zone and the quality of the vehicles they were selling—but it was only optimism for what they wanted to sell, not for what our needs were.

How about the discipline factor? They did very poorly on the basics. Combined with the poor performance in the other three areas, the probability of being successful, that is, making the sale, was very low.

Great Product, Weak Follow-Through. The automobile industry represents an integral part of our economy. When auto sales suffer our gross national product suffers drastically. Despite the number of foreign cars sold in the United States, our automobile industry still produces a fine product. The problem may be that the public doesn't perceive it as such.

Many automobile dealers have improved their once-impractical attitudes about service, and have created strong profit centers in their parts and service departments. In the area of service, the entire industry seems to have made a quantum leap forward.

However, the next time you shop for an automobile, grade the salesperson and see if he or she is using persuasive, high-energy techniques before you decide to hand over your money. If the techniques are not working on the salesroom floor, they may be equally absent in other areas of the business.

Now examine an objective overview of a salesperson using **Power Linguistic Sales Methodology**. He/she

- Builds rapport rapidly
- Asks many questions, and listens to responses
- Follows a sales methodology ("The System")
- Presents the company, product, or service after establishing and in response to customer needs
- Overcomes resistance, misinformation and bias
- Identifies and outsells competition
- Effects liaison—company-to-customer and customer-to-company
- Builds trust relationships

Now examine again Power Statements 4 and 5:

POWER STATEMENT #4: Selling is the least understood function within most companies.

POWER STATEMENT #5: Despite varying degrees of marketing success, many companies are inept in teaching or training salespeople to get the order (close the sale).

Not too dissimilar to the Audi salesperson described earlier. Many organizations rely on their brand and reputation, then infuse their sales personnel with overwhelming product information which they believe is what prospects and customers want to hear.

Most retail customers and a high percentage of industrial ones have needs that can only be discovered by processing and assessment. Poorly trained salespeople seldom uncover needs because they concentrate on wants. Although the words "need" and "want" are used interchangeably, they are completely different in both origin and purpose.

The simplest example I can give of the latter occurs when the prospect or customer raises price issues and the salesperson quickly assumes that they are looking for a lower-priced product or are attempting to negotiate an established price. While true in some cases, this assumption only accounts for a minority of the circumstances. The misinterpretation of phrases such as "Your price is too high," "That's too much money," and "I can do better than that" leads the poorly trained salesperson to actions that don't serve the best interests of the company or the customer.

In a study, we asked hundreds of customers who didn't buy from our clients what they wanted from their original contact with a salesperson; here is what our survey indicated. These prospects wanted:

Pricing (early)   Verification of beliefs
Quick solution   To procrastinate
Brief presentation   To control situation
Limited extras   Competitive price

When these same individuals were queried as to what their needs were in terms of the particular product/service, they unconsciously revealed portions of their value system, much of which may seem at odds with their original wants and begs for sales training, which responds to needs more than apparent wants. Observe the comparison; both findings came from the same study.

CUSTOMERS

WANTS	—VS—	NEEDS
Pricing (Early)		Information to Make Proper Decision
Quick Solution		Long Range Satisfaction
Brief Presentation		Complete Information
Limited Extras		Optional use
Verification of Beliefs		Factual, Verifiable Data
To Procrastinate		To Decide
To Control Situation		"Open" Relationships
Competitive Price		Exceptional Quality

In Power Linguistics Sales Training, salespeople are taught to process information received in such a way as to not offend prospects, customers, or even curious inquirers. They are taught early to assume nothing, ask questions to determine values, and even respond to questions with questions (the key to professional selling).

With Power Linguistic Training they ask questions such as, "Why do you say that?"

Each question asked is designed to obtain more information about what the prospect means. Other similar responses include: "What did you have in mind?" "Why do you feel that way?" "What gives rise to that opinion?" and "Run that by me one more time."

In this style of communication you answer questions or address statements with questions to obtain more precise information about what the customer is saying. When a customer says, "Your price is too high," what does that really mean? There are dozens of reasons for making the statement, and only two of them directly deal with price. Most of the reasons represent tactics the customer may be using (for example, some customers have learned to automatically cringe when a price is mentioned) or a condition they want fulfilled before buying.

When you respond to, "Your price is too high," with "Why do you say that?" customers usually redefine the answer:

Customer: "Your price is too high."
Salesperson: "Why do you say that?"
Customer: "Because . . ."

Our Power Linguistic surveys indicate the following (most likely) intent of some of the most common responses.

Response	Intent
"We're buying something for less."	Convince me yours is worth the difference.
"Everyone gives discounts."	A test or trial for a better price Needs convincing to upgrade

Response	Intent
"I hadn't seen this model before."	Needs more information or verification
"It's a lot more than we intended to spend."	Needs convincing to upgrade
"We're over our budget."	A test to gauge your response
"My authorization is limited."	No authority to buy above $X
"We like yours better, but we've got a lower price."	May want to negotiate
"My friend bought something similar last year for less."	Outdated information
"We'll wait for prices to come down."	Procrastination
"We can get it for less."	A test to see if you'll drop the price

Without this type of dialogue, the statement, "Your price is too high," is usually interpreted only from the salesperson's value system and viewpoint. Think for a moment. There are over 550,000 words in the modern dictionary, although most people use only 2 to 3 percent of them. Five hundred of the most commonly used words have several meanings. It stands to reason that different words may have veiled intent, certainly meanings other than your interpretation.

Once the customer is questioned using Power Linguistics processing and offers a new response, you derive a greater understanding of the prospect's values, goals, and feelings. You can then pose another question to the prospect's response to gain a greater insight as to how to serve him or her. At any time during a customer interaction the golden rule is: **When in doubt, ask another question.**

The trap in responding to most questions with an answer is that you will tend to use your own value system as a measurement, and unless your value system is the same as the prospect's, it creates a malfunction in the communication. For example, if the prospect says, "Which of these are the best?" and the salesperson says, "Here is the one I like," the salesperson is operating from his or her own value system.

Case #54: Resistance to Power Linguistic Language

I was conducting a seminar for engineers who specified and designed a product sold by sales engineers. When I presented the idea of power and neutral words, as well as high-energy words and phrases, there was immediate resistance. A sales engineer who was particularly vocal wanted to know, "How can I, as an engineer who is supposed to know my product, respond to another engineer with questions like, 'Why do you ask?' I think I would look foolish."

He had answered his own question. If the method would make him feel foolish, there is a strong possibility that he would not use it. In that same training session, we had Power Linguistic process questions written by each salesperson (in their own handwriting) on a series of three-by-five cards.

These sales engineers agreed to participate in using the system for twenty-one days only—accepting the early awkwardness, putting aside the ego problem of feeling foolish, and using the cards as reminders and cues. At the end of twenty-one days, the sales team had agreed to measure their effectiveness based on improved communications and increased sales activity.

Within thirty days we received a completed questionnaire from each participant. Based on their reporting, only 78 percent attempted the process at least once. Of those who attempted the process at least once only 40 percent used it for two weeks or more. Twenty-three percent experienced improved communications and felt it was contributing positively to their sales activity.

Most of the 23 percent were still using it at the time of the follow-up seminar. Best of all, the general manager of the division who had attended the earlier meeting used the practice with favorable results during union negotiations.

Power Linguistics communication, particularly processing, remains one of the most powerful techniques we use in training. Yet, without spaced repetition and the support of those charged with follow-through training or field management, this great method does not become a working tool for salespeople and others.

The ACID Test

The use of the acronym ACID can help you improve your power communication. By remembering the four letters A, C, I, and D you have an easy method to remember the steps to positive, powerful communication.

A   Arouse
C   Cultivate
I   Information
D   Determine

If I can arouse you sufficiently, then I can cultivate your interest, and you'll likely provide information that helps me to determine your needs and value system, and subsequently how to deal with you. If we communicate well and there are no misunderstandings in our communication, it is because I am talking about things that interest you, at a level of your awareness, with your goals and values in mind.

Most people reverse the ACID process and start with the D by making a determination about you, your goals and values based on how you look, what you've just said, and other minuscule cues.

Did They Buy or Were They Sold? Examine how ACID works in selling and how you know if you are communicating effectively with a prospect.

A sales presentation that is tailored to a prospect's needs, goals, values and feelings is viewed more favorably than one which is not. If you were to ask a friend where he bought his suit, appliance, or car, he would usually reply, "I bought it at X," or, "I bought it from Y." He is claiming credit for the purchase. He's not likely to say, "Y sold it to me," in which case credit for the transaction would go to the seller.

This is more than a play on words. It reveals the customer's perception of a transaction, and the skills of the seller.

Using the ACID technique enables the salesperson to make customers feel they bought, instead of being sold.

Arouse: Do you create early rapport with prospects and give them a desire to spend more time with you, your idea, or your product? The outcome of many buy-sell relationships is often based on what happens in the first two minutes in person, and in the first thirty seconds over the phone.

Cultivate: Do you cultivate the prospect's interest? Do you ask questions which induce prospects to talk about themselves and their goals, values, and feelings?

Information: Do you acquire sufficient information, and how did you remember it? Do you use the information to lead to additional questioning, which produces even more information? If you make multiple calls prior to attempting to sell or close, how and where did you catalogue the information?

Determine: Do you determine from the information you have how, when, and where you will make your presentation; what the prospect's goals, values, and needs are; and how you will fulfill them with your presentation?

Think about this sequence. If I arouse and cultivate you, and you give me the information that I need, that will help me determine how to deal with you.

ACID within a Nurturing Environment. There are essentially four motivational environments in which most buying decisions are made: gain, pride, fear, and imitation. Perhaps these are not the noblest of motivations, but being human our decision-making process often boils down to one of the four:

Gain: "What do I get out of it?"
Pride: "How does it make me look?"
Fear: "What will happen if I don't do it?"
Imitation: "Who else is doing it?"

If I'm trying to get you to buy, it is unwise to prejudge or stereotype your behavior. To be successful, I have to get as close as possible to standing in your shoes. When I ask your opinion on how you feel about certain issues, I need to listen and avoid value judgments and rapid determinations. This approach will enable me to create an environment where you will feel comfortable. While I may not be able to motivate everyone, I can create and stimulate an environment in which motivation may occur.

EPOD Tactics

- Stop telling; selling requires a lot of listening.
- Listening and processing information equates with helping and caring.
- Sell more per customer. Suppose you run a retail specialty store, and traditionally one out of every five people who come into the store end up buying. If you improve your skills and sell to one out of four people, you capture 25 percent rather than 20 percent of your prospects.
- Creative selling comes about when the buyer is convinced it is his decision to buy. Notice that the satisfied customer often says, "I bought it from . . . ," and seldom, "What's-his-name sold it to me."
- Retail advertising should not be treated as an art form that we stand around and admire. Sound advertising sells an idea and creates prospects. Then it's up to the individual salesperson to bring fulfillment by turning prospects into customers.
- Acknowledge that the power of an idea can be measured by the degree of resistance that it encounters. EPOD selling is directed at changing mind-sets.
- Write down ideas that you hear which you don't agree with or don't fit your value system. Then realize your customers go through the same process.
- Now, take the most compelling idea you listed and share it with a half-dozen people. Do they like the idea? Will they

use it, and when? You'll quickly see why it is difficult to sell ideas.
- Ideas are frequently rejected because they come from an outside source. To sell ideas to people, get them to see it as their own. Take the representational information* given by your prospects and build this into your presentation. This is not deception, but an effective form of packaging the idea using persuasive language.
- When presenting ideas to clients, use a resistance-reducing format. For example, "Bob, I saw your staff doing something, and it struck me that with a few modifications it could really pay off. Let me suggest the following." This technique integrates the idea with something that they are already doing. Using it is perceived as their idea being modified, not an idea different from theirs.
- Send a minimum of two to four reminders to clients, customers, and prospects annually; sending more frequently works even better.
- If you want to sell something other than by its low price, make an inventory of all things surrounding your product or service, and the people and equipment needed to support the product. Get to know your inventory and present it as part of your package before you quote the price. It reduces the perception of a higher price.
- Closing the sale is the natural conclusion to the successful completion of each step of a sound selling plan.
- To construct a methodology to sell more and more profitably, know the prospect and understand his/her value system.
- To improve communication remember the following:
    - Answer questions with questions.
    - Objections are a sign of interest.
    - The degree of intensity given to the objection measures the degree of its importance.

---

*Representational information is a form of psychological processing commonly used in neurolinguistic programming, counselor skill training and psychological counseling. It refers to anything that represents giver, sender or speaker's value system.

- The power of an idea can be measured by the degree of resistance it attracts.
- Technical questions do not always require technical answers.

• The next time you decide to market a low-price product or service that depends on volume, remember these three realities:

  1. Someone will always have a lower price.
  2. There will always be price objections.
  3. You will lose some orders to a lower price.

• I advise every high school or college student to experience door-to-door selling. There is no better way to build self-confidence and find out what the real world of buying and selling is all about.

CHAPTER 8

Applying the EPOD Theory in Business

"He that complies against his will is of his own opinion still."
—*Samuel Butler*

Leaders and managers are frequently selected early in their careers. Someone examines their education, experience, and behavioral style, then mentally stamps their resume with the words, "leadership qualities."

However, history eventually measures the degree of success that individuals attain. There are often highly specialized challenges facing the new leader/managers, and despite formal education, experience, and the support they receive, success eludes them.

A successful manager may not come equipped with the skills and behavior that seemingly accompany leadership as normally perceived.

Most political historians believe that Harry Truman lacked the polish and skills that would have been necessary to be elected to the presidency of the United States. The press, foreign dignitaries, fellow politicians, and a large percentage of the public often spoke of his lack of charisma, his blunt style of speaking, as well as his early connections to the Pendergast political machine in Missouri, which came under great criticism.

Truman inherited the office with the death of President Franklin Roosevelt, who having served fourteen years unquestionably left his imprimatur on the office. Our country was at war. There was little time for political finesse when it came to some of Truman's early decisions. Yet, history has shown he was one of the most effective presidents of the twentieth century.

A likewise comparison might be Alfred Sloan, who guided General Motors to its ascendance in its halcyon days. The list will grow when you measure accomplishment versus style. The media and a good portion of the public want Warren Buffet of Berkshire Hathaway and Bill Gates of Microsoft to fit the mold and stereotype of management that has been created by the media and revisionist historians.

Peter Drucker, in an article in the *Harvard Business Review*, calls on his sixty-five-plus years of consulting with and for some of the largest and most successful companies in the world to evaluate competent leadership.

Drucker, commenting on effective executives, stated:

> They were all over the map in terms of their personalities, attitudes, values, strengths, and weaknesses. They ranged from extroverted to nearly reclusive, from easygoing to controlling, from generous to parsimonious.

He then goes on to expostulate on the common practices that effective managers use to run enterprises. He said that the first two practices related to questions they asked: "What needs to be done?" and "What is right for the enterprise?"

These questions, Drucker said, gave them the knowledge they needed. From the responses they received, they developed action plans. Then they took responsibility for their decisions. They also took responsibility for communicating these decisions. They stayed focused on opportunities rather than problems. These later practices helped them convert acquired knowledge into effective action.

Two additional practices that Drucker observed were: They ran productive meetings and they thought and said "we" rather than "I." These practices ensured that the whole organization felt both responsible and accountable. Observe how these practices are synergistic and how they fit into the EPOD Theory.

The practice of EPOD Management Techniques requires that old stereotypes, bromides, and out-of-date thinking get scrapped.

Here is what may seem like an abstract example:

My maternal grandfather was a hard-working laborer who at the time of his death owned a home, had no debt, and had provided for his wife, who had diabetes, glaucoma, and went blind—long before employers provided health insurance. He never had formal schooling, never made more than $40 a week, had only marginal social security benefits (remember it had its inception in 1935), and received approximately $20 per month as pension.

I learned important principles by listening to and observing him. Although he could neither read nor write, he lived by very simple practices, and I believe if all negotiating and contracting carried those principles, there would be fewer breakdowns in relationships. I know for sure that there would be less litigation:

- Don't spend more than you earn.
- Save something out of every paycheck.
- Never give your word unless you mean it.
- Never shake on a deal unless you intend to do what you say.
- If it's not yours, don't touch it.

If these seem like archaic principles, it is arguably because of a change in societal values, which promote everyone for themselves and you'd better grab what you can get while you can. However, I have had numerous clients who followed these simple practices to build their business.

The differences between Drucker's examples of management/leadership and my grandfather's philosophy may seem worlds apart. They are both, however, plans and practices by which individuals choose to lead their life and/or their companies.

We attract clients, many of whom have no set plan or practices in place, and yet somehow they run their business. Most, however, reach a level where a plan and practices have to be spelled out or they cannot grow their business.

The late J. Willard Marriott, founder of the hotel and restaurant chain that bears his name, wrote what he called "guideposts for managing" when he turned the presidency of the company over to his son. He stated that the principles and practices were "all born out of my experience and ones I wish I could have followed more closely."

Here are a few practices excerpted from his guideposts:

- Study and follow professional management principles. Apply these principles logically and practically to your organization.
- People grow by making decisions and assuming responsibility for them. Make crystal clear what decision each manager is responsible for and what decisions you reserve for yourself.
- Have all the facts and counsel necessary; then decide and stick to it.
- If inefficiency exists and it cannot be overcome and an employee is obviously incapable of the job, find a job he can do or terminate *now*. Don't wait.
- Know what your competitors are doing and planning.
- Encourage all management to think about better ways and give suggestions on anything that will improve business.
- Spend time and money on research and development.
- Delegate and hold managers accountable for results.
- See the good in people and try to develop those qualities. People are number one. Their development, loyalty, interest, and team spirit are primary considerations.
- Develop managers in every area. This is your prime responsibility.

Most of these practices seem easy to understand and implement. Why, then, do business owners and managers have endless excuses as to why they don't have a basic plan or list of practices by which to run their business? Rather than give you my perception of why, I challenge you to an EPOD test.

Make a short list of certain plans and practices for running your business, association, committee, family. or personal life. Next measure each element and the plan itself in four ways:

1. How much **energy** will I contribute to this?
2. How **persuasive** will I be in convincing others that these practices are in the best interest of our organization and the individual?
3. How **optimistic** am I that the plan and practice will work, and how will I convey my optimism to others?
4. How **disciplined** will I be in sticking with the principles of the plan and practices?

Grade yourself on a scale of 1 (low) to 10 (high). Be objective. Measure yourself over regular periods. Determine how you are doing in each area. Don't be harsh on yourself if one part of the plan is more difficult than the others. If one element of the plan or practice is not making the grade, you may need to modify or intensify your efforts.

As a company grows, its people have to grow with it, and they need a clear definition as to what is expected of them. Eventually, all business plans have to be stimulated into action. Here is where the definition of expectation comes into play. When a plan is translated into action, management has to pay specific attention to the decision-making model as well as the way the principles are communicated and how the outcome will translate to opportunities.

Again quoting Peter Drucker: "A decision has not been made until people know: The name of the person accountable for carrying it out; the deadline; the names of the people who will be affected by the decision and therefore have to know about, understand, and approve it—or at least not be strongly opposed to it; and the names of the people who have to be informed of the decision, even if they are not directly affected by it."

Contracts

Those who operate businesses today face myriad issues in which they may have little background or training. Despite a desire to be fair and honest and treat customers and employees in a manner that encourages satisfaction, managers have to broaden their knowledge in many areas that their counterparts of fifty years ago had no need to pursue.

Examine the manner in which contracts are negotiated and the value of contractuality. The following scenario is not uncommon.

A young athlete signs with a major sports franchise. His agent (often a lawyer) negotiates a three-year contract stating how the athlete will be paid, and that in turn, he will give his best effort. The athlete has a better year than anticipated so his agent says, "You are worth more than we bargained for. Don't report to training camp; hold out." Is this action justified because no one knew at the time that the athlete was going to be so great? Is he entitled to more? The prevailing wisdom seems to be that the action is justified because he is a more valuable asset than originally anticipated.

What does contractually mean? Essentially it means **you give your word**. Most breakdowns in contract relations are based on the integrity levels of the negotiating parties. To improve the outcome of your contracting may require being clear about

- Whom you are doing business with and what their standards are.
- What each side needs to make the transaction win-win.
- What each side anticipates as an outcome.
- Whether future issues will radically affect the agreement.

An Oath Is an Oath. During the Nixon administration there were more than one hundred public servants investigated or indicted for malfeasance (most were lawyers). Each had taken an oath to represent the best interests of our country and its citizens. Yet, even the then—Attorney General proclaimed, "I have done nothing illegal, unethical maybe, but not illegal." In later years President Clinton would seek to "parse" a response to the question of honesty by questioning the interpretation of the word "is."

A judge once told me that the courts do not decide cases on issues of ethics or morality. He was, of course, correct. However, I am not so sure that this was our founding fathers' intent in the original construction of our laws, and it may be a key ingredient as to why our legal system is breaking down. For in truth, when you leave morality and ethics out of your negotiations, most contracts and the relationships of the parties inevitably fail.

In Business, to Exploit Is to Lose

Those with extensive negotiation skills have many opportunities each year to take advantage of others with whom they negotiate. Because of their experience, they can predetermine how to structure a deal that turns out to be highly favorable for them and not so favorable for the other party.

However, when you enter into agreements that do not benefit both parties, ultimately the other party is going to be unhappy and may begin to dishonor parts of the agreement. Then no one benefits.

> When you negotiate to get your best deal to the detriment of the other party, the agreement is ultimately going to fail.

If I lease space to you, or I sell you something under terms and conditions that are onerous, biased, or overly burdensome, eventually you may try to find a way to circumvent the agreement or otherwise create a condition of malfunction. At the very least you may decide to become confrontational in other areas of our relationship.

Case #67. Intoxicating Negotiations

Years back, I had a client who would set up meetings with vendors at a posh restaurant. Dinner would be preceded and followed by considerable drinking. A nondrinker himself, his strategy was to get the other party so inebriated that when they began negotiating, the other party would give away the store.

I observed these dinner meetings a couple of times but felt uncomfortable. With vendors on their third martini, it certainly created an unfair negotiating advantage. I pondered about the long-term health of my client's business relations with those vendors.

> When you negotiate with the other party in mind, you are transmitting a message to them that how they fare is as important to you as how you fare in this relationship, and you get a stronger agreement from the standpoint of both parties honoring the agreement over the long run.

Case #33: Give and Take

When I was president of a conglomerate, my company had an annual contract with a major manufacturer to purchase materials from them at an agreed-upon price. We were one of their largest customers. Five months into the contract, their vice president asked to meet with me to discuss something important.

I arrived the evening before and met him for breakfast the next morning. He said, "We've looked at our existing contract with you and found that we really can't make a fair profit for the price per unit that you agreed to pay."

I could have essentially said to him, "You made your bed, now lie in it; we'll talk when this contract comes up for renewal." He would still supply me but be unhappy about it. Or, I could have said, "Okay, you've pushed me over a barrel, but just remember you owe me."

My business was growing, and I wanted to have a solid, long-term relationship with this important supplier. I said, "Tell me the amount you need." He said, "20 cents per unit," and explained the reasoning behind this request. I picked up a pad and wrote down some figures. I already knew what I was going to do. I said, "I'll give you 25 cents."

He was taken aback. "Wait a second, I said I only needed 20 cents."

I said, "I know, I'm offering 25."

He said, "Why?"

I said, "Tell me how much time that buys me."

He said, "Three years."

First, I got a long-term commitment, and he got an immediate price increase in excess of what was needed. When he reported to his president, who had a reputation for being a tough negotiator, I knew that this VP could play the hero. I could almost hear the words in their conference room, "If Yoho is willing to offer us 5 cents more when we didn't ask for it, he's got to be for real." Later in the year I asked for special dating on invoices that permitted my company to increase volume and still take prompt payment discounts. I received an approval within hours.

What would that VP remember about our negotiation? That in a moment of need I was not only fair, I was generous. In turn, when I expressed a need, he became generous with me.

Recognizing the Value Systems of Others in Negotiating

Everyone whom you encounter has a value system that is detectable if you listen and observe them long enough. If you sell a product or service, when someone questions your price, you may think that they are reflecting a value system. However, this is often a tactic.

If you observe that the person with whom you are negotiating has an expensive watch or clothing, or a high-priced automobile, you may be getting a glimpse of a value system, though that doesn't necessarily mean they would not negotiate to buy these things at a lower price. The person wearing a Rolex watch may have determined to get the top-of-the-line instrument because he placed a high value on style, looks, prestige, and so on. If price was the only issue, he might be wearing an inexpensive digital watch.

> Values are established by listening and evaluating responses and actions before you actually negotiate. What may seem like simple social conversation can have great impact on what you will say during negotiations.

Whenever you negotiate, do so only after identifying someone's value system. Then make your offer and presentation in accordance with what you know.

A Caveat. An established, irrefutable fact about negotiation is that if the other person places a low value on truth, ethics, or integrity, your negotiation will have little meaning, no matter what form it takes, and frequently you will be in for disappointing consequences.

Case #98: The Spoken Word Takes Precedence

I originally met Mel Rosenblatt just after he had become the new vice president of sales for a large, but struggling company. High volume and low profitability had his company on the ropes. He sought my company's account because we would become one of his largest customers.

After we became his customer, we negotiated on little more than a handshake and four paragraphs in a letter that would determine our annual relationship. When conditions arose that had to be addressed, we were always able to handle them over the phone. I never once had a falling out, disagreement, or condition wherein I felt he went back on his word.

Over many years our business relationship has changed. He has been a client in several different companies in different industries. Everyone who knows Mel gives him high marks for the way he keeps his word. I've learned that his reputation is the means by which he negotiates for new business and retains old customers at every level of his business.

I have negotiated long and complex situations involving great sums with him in the span of ten minutes on the telephone. My degree of trust in him is so great that I would play poker with him over the phone.

A Place for Honest Negotiations and Agreements. If honesty is important to you, you don't need to declare it; simply practice being honest. You may think to yourself, *Forget it, because the world is basically dishonest.* Yes, societal values in the United States have changed over the years, and being honest won't necessarily increase the probability of encountering other honest people. However, based on the concept of reciprocation, you may be surprised at the number of people who will react honestly in return.

I have frequently heard executives in large companies opine, "Why stick my neck out for a value that fewer and fewer people care about anyway?" My response is, "If that's your attitude, you may become a high achiever; however, if you sacrifice integrity for rapid success, the foundation of your achievement will always be shaky." Maintaining the status quo, adopting peer group values, or rationalizing makes for a mediocre career and life. Many of the corporate failures, executive indictments, and tarnished images you read about had their seeds in the rationalization of values.

Most of the great achievers I know have the courage to establish a set of values from which they do not back off.

The world is full of people who diverted funds, perhaps early in their careers, and went on to become very successful, only to have their earlier transgressions exposed and watch everything come tumbling down.

Case #191: Fraud Is Never Worth the Price

Some years ago a businessman who pleaded guilty to defrauding the government ran a full-page ad in *The Philadelphia Inquirer* titled, "An Open Letter of Apology." In it, he noted that he had lost his business, health, and family as a result of his offense.

He urged others to learn a lesson from his mistakes. "Don't make the almighty dollar the guiding force for your business decisions," he said. "Instead, for every business decision you make, ask yourself: Is what I am doing right?"

He closed with this message for young people considering business careers: "The true measure of success is not your financial worth, but how much you are worth to your friends, family, community and most of all to yourself. Right now I don't feel like I'm worth very much." (from *Communication Briefings*, reprinted with permission)

Frequently, when I submit a proposed agreement to someone, that person will take my document to his or her lawyer. Invariably, we have to explain the conditions to the lawyer. Sometimes it's simple and other times we are required to extend the length of the agreement and the ideas which we agreed upon in the first place. Frequently, the cost increases without any benefit to either party.

Short and Sweet. Is your ability to have a satisfactory contractual relationship directly related to the length of the contract? It often seems the longer and more involved the agreement, the less probable that you will have a viable, long-term relationship.

While all of the important issues have to be covered, when an agreement gets too long, it is frequently because someone is trying to obscure the terms of the relationship.

Case #25: Too Long Means Things Will Go Wrong

Once when I was seeking to acquire a sizable business, during our due diligence we were shown a new and lengthy lease. In this closely held business, the principals of the company owned the building in their own name and leased the premises back to the business.

The negotiations had been lengthy. Closing day was held on a Saturday as a convenience to me because I was returning from out of town. My attorney had come several hours before I was scheduled to arrive. It was then that the lease was submitted.

The lease submitted consisted of thirty-two pages! My attorney highlighted all the clauses and phrases of concern to us. (I found out later that the parties assembled that morning had spent hours just on the lease provisions.) I had expected to close quickly, but this was not the case.

I asked to review the lease, which required about forty-five minutes, and then asked the seller's attorney why it was so complicated.

Attorney: "It's a standard lease that we draw up."
Me: "Let me see the lease they used previously."

Attorney: "We can, but that lease no longer applies."
Me: "They had to have the same protection that we want, so let's use that lease."

Attorney: "Sorry, we can't."
Me: "Well, just tell me how long was that lease."

Attorney: "I don't remember."
Me: "Was it thirty pages?"

Attorney: "No I don't think so."
Me: "Then, why does this have thirty-two pages?"

Attorney: "You are going to be taking over their building, and I've included additional protections."

I reminded the attorney that when we negotiated to acquire this company, we were aware of this leaseback arrangement. In fact, we had offered to buy the building. He wouldn't budge. I said, "I don't think we're going to proceed with the deal. There are clauses which I'm sure are not necessary, and they weren't disclosed in our earlier negotiations."

He said, "I am representing my client, and this is what I advise them to do."

I said, "Fine but we're not doing business. Anything that takes thirty-two pages is not in my company's best interest. We haven't acquired the company or even moved into the building and you present unforeseen problems. I perceive that it is in our best interest to bow out now."

I'm sure their attorney knew we had the funds for closing in our bank, borrowed from an institution, and that there would be costs to us when we returned the funds—plus all of our legal bills. Yet I thanked the attorneys and adjourned the meeting.

Their attorney got flushed and said, "Mr. Yoho, you are being petulant."

I said to him, "That may be, but I've learned that if an agreement becomes tacky or burdensome at the outset, it's only going to get worse later." I also reminded him that the Declaration of Independence is a short document developed by many people with clarity and thoughtfulness. It created an independent country—and it didn't take thirty-two pages.

Don't Be Intimidated at Real Estate Closings. When you purchase real estate you are besieged with fifteen to twenty documents involving dozens of clauses. The typical person will not completely read all these documents and will frequently regret it later. Here is a suggestion: request a copy of all documents then read them in advance of the closing.

> It takes time to understand the terms so that you can buy a piece of property and sign the appropriate documents with intelligence and peace of mind.

What if it takes several hours to read these documents? You may not feel like you have the necessary time to devote to these matters, but how better could you be spending your time than carefully reviewing the terms of contracts that you are about to sign? How important is it for you to understand and confirm the purchases, sales, or relationships that you enter into in your life?

The Keys to Working with Lawyers, Accountants, and Consultants

My grandmother was from Estonia, in Eastern Europe. There is an old Baltic curse: "May your life be filled with lawyers." We have become a litigious society. There are over 1 million lawyers in the United States alone. This equates to an average of one lawyer for every 250 adults. Japan, with a population half our size, has approximately 130,000 lawyers.

The lawyer glut contributes to a situation where many aggressively reach for business, creating an atmosphere of fear and distrust, and an abdication of sound ethics and morals in our business and personal lives. Certainly we need legal advice.

However, when working with or through lawyers, one often notices a working style that leads to confrontation and the abuse of your time, energy, and funds. Cases are extended, troubles are manufactured, and things become much more complicated than they need to be.

I advise my clients to:

- Shop for an attorney who meets your needs.
- Check their references. Ask to speak to bankers, landlords, and suppliers. Check them out the same as with any vendor.
- Check on their specialties. In most small or moderate-sized businesses, you may be better off working with two or three small firms rather than one large one.
- Ask for complete information on fees and other pricing factors, and get it in writing.
- Ask for the names of previous clients, and *call them*. Ask for details such as promptness, courtesy, follow-through, how the services were used, level of satisfaction, and whether they would use the lawyers again. (Keep in mind, you probably won't be given the names of "problem" clients.)
- Evaluate how the attorney asks questions of you and what he feels is important to know about you and your business.

Using Attorneys in Your Best Interest

While a high percentage of the advice that small business entrepreneurs receive from lawyers and accountants may not be in their best interest, often it is because the entrepreneur doesn't provide the professional with total information on the business and how it is run.

You, not your lawyer, are responsible for maintaining goals, acknowledging changes that occur, and coming up with effective decisions. Too often when entrepreneurs take a contract or a proposed strategy to counsel they unwittingly engage in deal breaking rather than deal making. The counsel, who may not know all the facts, tells you to proceed or not.

At the same time, don't use the professional as a whipping boy. Many people wait until a situation develops or sours and then say, "Well, my accountant or lawyer told me to do it [not do it] and that's where I went wrong." Decisions are ultimately yours. As you become responsible for them and their outcomes, your decision-making process will improve.

Working with Accountants

Much of what has been discussed about working with a lawyer applies to working with an accountant. The key factor is that the accountant does not make business decisions for you, but rather advises you of the status of your business based on the review of your financial documents and situations. The accountant can point out, for example, possible tax liabilities or the need for working capital.

Taking Responsibility. Don't get in the habit of counting on accountants (or any other retained professional) to do things that they are not qualified to do or can't do. For example, your accountant cannot effectively document transactions for you.

> The palest ink is better than the most remarkable memory. Anything you do in business has to be documented by you. It can be as simple as sending a memo to yourself or creating a computer file. Once you create it, you can have someone review the document or memo.

The lack of documentation in business is widespread. People enter into agreements, borrow money, sign notes, and complete transactions without establishing a backup paper trail. Without documentation of what you do, your exposure multiplies.

If your answer is, *I can't document everything, I am overwhelmed*, then don't proceed, or proceed with the realization that you are taking unneeded risk. It won't serve you later to say, "I did not know that clause was included," or "I did not know I had to file that application or report."

Hiring and Dealing with Consultants

Consulting, in its purest context, implies "working together." If this relationship is your proposed goal, then consider some of the issues you will have to deal with and some methods that work better than others.

Most established consultants have a list of clients, and some have unsolicited recommendation letters. To make a wise decision, suggest that the potential consultant provide you with a list of his last three or four assignments, including the principal with whom he or she is dealing in the client company.

Solicit Feedback. Have a prepared list of questions when calling the references, and try to follow a prescribed method in soliciting feedback information. Although the following list was prepared for researching and evaluating a consultant, many of the same questions apply if the party being considered is a lawyer or accountant.

1. How long had you known the consultant prior to retaining him/her?
2. How long has the client-consultant relationship been in existence?
3. Was the consultant hired for a specific project(s)? What outcome were you seeking (anticipating) when you retained the consultant?
4. Was the project completed in the prescribed time constraints? On a scale of 1 (low) to 10 (high), how would you rate the outcome (or current effect of the consultant)?
5. [If the project has been completed] Would you retain the consultant again?
6. What is your opinion of the consultant's style? (Listen carefully for feedback. You will hear information relating to the way the consultant identified with members of the client's company, customers, etc.)
7. Did you acquire critique sheets from those working with the consultant, and if so, what was the general opinion?

PROS ↑ AND CONS ↓
FOR HIRING CONSULTANTS
(Sampling From Executives Who Regularly Hire Consultants)

↑ When you consider payroll costs (F.I.C.A., F.U.T.A., vacations, hospitalization, etc.), their cost is frequently lower—much lower.

↑ If the consultant has broad industry experience, it's like having a research department.

↓ if a consultant isn't a quick study, you may be paying for "on-the-job training".

↑ Many consultants have executive experience beyond those of the company they serve.

↔ Consultants frequently represent a threat to employees, managers and executives egos.

↓ If they don't unearth problems and issues beyond their assignment they are of limited value.

↑ Their departure, even when a cancellation proviso is invoked, is always less costly than most severance packages.

↑ If you have the "rights" to tape (audio or video) you benefit from the continuing use of the information provided.

↓ Don't treat them like employees by including them in every function or you may forget why you hired an independent thinker.

↑ Many consultants have the ability to spark up and ignite meetings/training sessions. It's like having an informed motivator on your staff.

(The main thrust of this exercise is to analyze compatibility to your project or organization.)

Next, meet and talk with the consultant to assess compatibility with you, your project, and your organization. Clearly define what is expected of each other with an informal agreement. Consider whether your associates will be able to relate to this consultant; will the consultant be able to adapt to the culture of your organization?

Interview in Person. Many consultants have an "observation fee" which enables the client to both interview and get information at the same time. This maximizes time and personal resources, and enables the client to evaluate styles and methods in terms of compatibility. The observation fee charged by the consultant covers the cost of a few hours of his/her time and obviates the client's feeling of obligation while presenting an ideal opportunity to measure the consultant's skill. Then make a go/no-go decision.

Define the Anticipated Outcome. Clearly define what is expected of each other with an informal contract. This can be something as simple as notes on a scratch-pad as an aftermath of your preparatory session, with each party initialing identical copies of the notes.

For more involved projects, exchange letters in advance that clearly define meetings, agendas, content, confidentiality provisos, time parameters, fees and expense reimbursement arrangements, and so on. This will avoid most misunderstandings during representation. While some consultants have a formal contract, many do not. Remember: the palest ink is better than the most remarkable memory.

EPOD Tactics

Integrity in negotiations:

- If you have a problem with fees quoted or proposed, try this: "I believe your price is fair because you seem like a fair person to me, so I'll be equally fair with you. Here is my problem: [state it]. If you can help me solve it, I believe we can do business." **The latter works a lot better than a contrived machination.**

- If you are a great negotiator or salesperson, don't take advantage of people. Structure arrangements that work for both parties. It will require personal discipline, however, to keep yourself in check.
- If you expect the consultant to function as a member of the team, providing detailed input information will be extremely important to the outcome.
- Whenever possible, *write it down*, even if it is three paragraphs on ruled paper. Date it, initial it, and ask each party to take a copy. When you renegotiate, pull out your original agreements.
- If you strike an agreement over the phone, confirm it by email, fax, or letter. Be brief but distinct. Ask the other party to read it, initial it, and return it.
- Most advice from professional sources comes with a price tag. Once received, consider these options:

  - Listen carefully to all aspects of the input, and then do nothing about it.
  - Take the advice and ideas, then modify or vary them before you utilize them.
  - Take the advice and ideas and alter them to the extreme so that they no longer resemble their original form.

  OR

  - Take the ideas as they are given, experiment with them, utilize them, and make progress or profit from the exchange. In any case, the advice costs the same.

- A lawyer is running a business. Evaluate carefully: who benefits most from the advice you receive, you or the lawyer?
- Remember that a lawyer's business is giving legal advice; however, many really want to give personal and business advice. Check their business habits or personal lives if you intend to take the nonlegal advice they offer.

- The next time you visit your attorney, accountant, consultant, medical doctor, dentist, or any other professional service provider:
    - Grade him or her on interaction skills.
    - Determine how you really feel about the service provided.

These professionals serve you in a technical capacity, and the quality of those skills is important. Added to that, why not find out how much they care about you as a person, and whether you feel good about your interaction with them?

CHAPTER 9

Movers and Shakers

"Some lead a quiet blameless life.
For them there are few terrors.
St. Peter will write the final score.
No hits, no runs, no errors."
—*Anonymous*

Movers and shakers are usually risk takers. Many times they are those who have in some way been deprived. They frequently lead by confidence in the belief that there is a better way and a better tomorrow for themselves and others. What others consider a handicap, they accept as an opportunity.

The four elements of EPOD were empirically drawn from research and the observation of people who are movers and shakers, those who exemplify high energy, persuasiveness, optimism, and discipline.

Many years ago when Lee Iacocca engineered a turnaround at Chrysler, funds were not available for model changes, plant expansion, retooling, or abundant advertising. One of the brilliant leadership characteristics that Iacocca exhibited was dictating major changes in the company and then selling vendors, dealers, and customers on those changes.

When he sold Chrysler's tank plant in Lima, Ohio (against the advice of his financial advisors), he was able to generate immediate cash. Interviewed on television that evening, he used persuasive language about the future of Chrysler by stating that the company had more money in its treasury than at any time in the last several years. This gesture greatly raised the confidence level of Chrysler employees who were justifiably concerned about the stability of the company, receiving their next paycheck, or receiving their pension and retirement benefits.

Iacocca's persuasiveness bolstered the confidence of suppliers who feared that they might not get paid. He increased the confidence of Chrysler dealers and customers, the people who sold and bought Chrysler products. With his own energy and persuasiveness Iacocca became a mover and shaker for an organization peopled by those who seriously doubted the company's ability to survive.

What about Iacocca's style transmits high energy and persuasiveness? For one, he can't speak without moving his hands. Also, whomever he addresses, whether it's a television audience, union negotiators, an assembly hall, or a boardroom group, he looks them straight in the eye. Furthermore, he speaks in an upbeat, assuring manner such that the logic (or lack of logic) seems immediately apparent.

When he presented Chrysler's five-year, fifty-thousand-mile warranty, he made it the backbone of his television advertising pitches. Many people who saw the ad bought the concept, yet who stopped and questioned that the CEO of a virtually bankrupt company was offering five-year warranties?

Chrysler couldn't compete with Ford or General Motors by offering a radically different car or by building a new plant. Chrysler products would have had little chance in a head-to-head, traditional advertising campaign. However, the radical innovation of Iacocca's "buyer protection plan" shook up the auto industry. Later, he extended Chrysler's offering by introducing the "car buyer's bill of rights." These were programs positioned to persuade customers of Chrysler's dependability, while at the same time making Chrysler dealers competitive to General Motors and Ford.

Chrysler was still one of the big three in the U.S. automobile industry, but their market share was minuscule compared to General Motors and Ford. For Chrysler, the weak third sister of the U.S. auto industry, to take the lead in offering buyer incentives was tantamount to the tail wagging the dog. It is obvious, after the fact, that these actions conveyed optimism to the company's employees, vendors, and customers.

Getting Things Done Uniquely

Some classic movers and shakers from recent history were Mahatma Gandhi, Mother Teresa, and Martin Luther King Jr. Gandhi changed all the rules, confronting the British with his brand of passive resistance and civil disobedience. Gandhi used these and other tools at his disposal—the written word, masses of devoted followers, and world opinion—to manipulate the British in ways that eventually led to India's independence.

Dr. King emulated Gandhi's techniques. In the early 1960s I lived in the Northeast and regarded myself as a typical white, middle-class American. I didn't understand all the issues about civil rights, and candidly some of the maneuvers used on both sides of the civil rights struggle annoyed me. Nevertheless, I recognized that Dr. Martin Luther King and African Americans had an important cause that wasn't getting resolved by political action, law enforcement, or violence.

In a major incident, Dr. King and his followers were confronted by Bull Connor, then police chief of Birmingham, Alabama. The civil rights advocates led by Dr. King and his followers were harassed by fierce police dogs, yet chose to sit down and not resist. When the opposition used billy clubs and tear gas, King and his followers still did not resist. When the opposition threatened an attack that might lead to death, Dr. King said, "We will love you with our dying breath."

When I saw Martin Luther King on television tell his followers, "Do not resist," "Do not fight back," and "Do not raise your hand," I knew he would prevail. He was embodying the most powerful Judeo-Christian philosophy of nonviolence; he had already won.

In my speaking career, I had frequent opportunities to work with Dr. Norman Vincent Peale. Anyone who observed Dr. Peale at work readily observed the tremendous energy he brought to his public appearances. When he was ninety-one years old, he still maintained a vigorous daily schedule. Peale had a deep sincerity about his work, and this was at the root of his messages. For over fifty years he was the pastor at Marble Collegiate Church in New York City.

One of the great religious leaders in the world, Peale led a life that served as a shining example to his congregation and followers. He was upbeat, energetic, and filled with optimism, and he had a persuasive style that affected the lives of millions.

Movers and Shakers in Business. You don't have to be a part of history, put your life on the line, or have thousands of followers to be a mover and shaker; you can become one within your own organization or within your business.

Case #46: You Give, You Get

> "Perhaps miracles obey laws that we humans generally do not understand."
> —M. Scott Peck, The Road Less Traveled

Norman Rales's story unfolds like a Damon Runyon novel. In 1923, Norman, who was three years old, along with his two brothers and one sister became wards of the State of New York and residents of an orphanage at 137th Street and Amsterdam Avenue in New York City. His mother had recently passed away from the birth of his last sister, and his grieving immigrant father, with little education and even fewer skills, believed that these children would have better opportunities as wards of the state than he could provide.

As Norman tells it, life in the orphanage was bearable. While you didn't have a mother or father to touch, talk to, and love, at least someone saw to it that you had a bed and were schooled, and that your daily needs were met. For fourteen years this was home for him and his siblings.

On his eighteenth birthday, with a toothbrush and $5 from the City of New York, he was told it was now his time to go into the world and become self-sufficient. He remembers being told, "The whole U.S. is yours. Go find what you want to do." So in 1939, without ever having completed high school, he and his friend Danie hopped a freight train and worked their way to California. His resume is replete with the titles of waiter, busboy, dishwasher, ditch digger, truck driver, shipyard worker, and carnival roustabout.

It was in this latter occupation that his travels took him to Florida and he met his wife, Ruth, who he married in 1948. She complemented and mentored the drive of this errant soul and encouraged him to become a door-to-door salesman for a home products company in Pittsburgh, Pennsylvania. The job required the use of a car, and although he had no credit background and lived in an apartment with little furniture, at the age of twenty-eight he went into the Mellon Bank to borrow money for a car.

The loan officer, E. Dudley Townsend, took a risk in giving a loan to this young man with no capital, few assets, and obviously no collateral. Later Dudley Townsend would become president of one of the corporations that Norman Rales owned.

Norman Rales is a mover and shaker nonplused. He commutes between his offices in Boca Raton, Florida, and Potomac, Maryland, in his own piloted Lear jet. He owns or has owned a bank; part interest in the Texas Rangers baseball team; the well-known resort in French Lick, Indiana; and the Golden Strand and Hollywood Beach Hotels in Florida, and several lesser-known hotels. He held majority interests in both public and private corporations such as Master Shield, a company called VIPCO, a chain of a building supply companies, and a finance company.

His success is based on simple, yet basic principles. Norman describes it as, "Givin' is gettin'." When his first business became successful, Dan, his boyhood friend, was invited to participate in ownership.

Norman Rales believes in returning to those who aided him. Several of the businesses that he founded became

ESOP companies, ultimately making employees the owners, and even making the truck drivers independently wealthy.

In 1979 Norman sought the eleven men from the orphanage who as boys had played on a championship basketball team together and brought them together for a reunion. One year later he started taking them and their families on an annual trip abroad to places like Rome, Paris, and Switzerland. Several years later he asked them to help find the people who had been in the same orphanage (since razed with few existing records); then he invited them to a party at the Bahia Mar Yacht Club in Ft. Lauderdale, Florida. The party, which took place on the Sunday between the NFL Championship and the Super Bowl, started with approximately fifty people. Now it has become an annual event, which over five hundred people attend.

Norman Rales's concept of "Givin' is gettin'" is based on a **strong business philosophy of making everyone you meet your partner**. His actions seem the antithesis of someone who could be perceived as being deserted as a child. Norman Rales epitomizes the American dream: a strong work ethic, a great dreamer, a lover of humanity, and a man who nurtures those around him.

His orphanage friend and companion Art Buchwald received the Horatio Alger Award in May 1989 in Washington, D.C. It is not coincidental that these men prospered, even though they started out with much less than the average individual. When you applaud their accomplishments remember that somewhere, someone else (possibly you) is saying, "If only I had a better start, more direction, more loving parents, some assets to begin with, or a stronger role model, I could have made it."

The Common Denominators

How do you become a mover and shaker right where you are? Find a way to excel. Learn more about your job than anyone else, and learn about the jobs of others around you. Compensate for what you do not presently know about the job by exhibiting higher levels of enthusiasm, excitation, and dedication.

Being loyal to the people you work for is also an important initial step on your road to becoming a mover and shaker. When bosses and top managers know that you are loyal, they tend to be more confident in you. Unfortunately, loyalty seems to be becoming a lost art in the workplace today.

Begin transmitting high energy to your coworkers, and you will soon be regarded as someone with leadership potential.

Personality Plus. Becoming a mover and shaker often requires developing a unique style, and indeed, many businesses assume the style of their leader and thereby accomplish what advertising and selling cannot do on their own.

To become a mover and shaker, develop your unique style and transfer it to your business (or your position).

When Frank Perdue said, "It takes a tough man to raise a tender chicken," he was perceived as having personal involvement in rearing the chicken you may buy next week. The business he founded and guided to national prominence bore his personal imprimatur in virtually every aspect of its activity.

Tom Carvel, who headed the ice cream company bearing his name, would not seem to have the voice, diction. or stage presence to be a radio or television announcer. Yet he perfected the art of starring in his own commercials, without appearing visually, and lending credibility and reliability to his product.

When J. C. Penney said that the quality of the suits and shirts in his stores were unparalleled, he backed up his statement by always wearing a blue suit and white poplin shirt that came out of stock. In the halcyon days of the J.C. Penney Company, his simple concepts of "value given for money spent" and his appeal to the common man through his own lifestyle made him a mover and shaker.

If you are just starting your career, to make it in a climate in which people say, "You don't have any experience," you say, "Hire me, I am willing to work harder and do more than the average applicant. Check me out." Then work harder and do more.

Movers and Shakers Are Innovators. Keep an eye on ways that you can become an innovator. In your job or your department is there something that can be done faster, smoother, more efficiently? Even the most well-established and conservative organizations appreciate innovation when it leads to greater profits, reduced costs, or enhanced operations. In most growing organizations there are numerous opportunities to innovate right where you are.

Case #113: Idea of the Week

Ira Hayes, former vice president of advertising at National Cash Register and head of their speakers bureau for many years, strongly believed that success emanated from an "idea per week."

At thousands of meetings where he was speaking, Hayes displayed his large three-ring binder, replete with rumpled pages, containing each of his "ideas of the week." He believed that by writing down one new idea each week, many become implanted and accelerate the growth and progress of the "idea accumulator."

The movers and shakers of tomorrow are those who have the resolve to write down an idea, despite its source, and to keep trying it, despite resistance they may encounter.

Many large organizations do not appear overly risk-oriented or open to change, particularly in relation to simple things such as the dress code and decorum of staff in the public eye. However, that doesn't mean large organizations don't appreciate innovation from the troops. Don't confuse an organization's desire to maintain a dress code or strict standard of performance with its eagerness to have creative, innovative thinkers on staff.

Regardless of the size of your organization, if you show upper management a better way—a more appealing package, a less costly distribution system, a more appropriate service mix, or a more comfortable, flexible, or salable product—they may listen.

Uninhibited by Opinions. In most organizations it won't be managers who inhibit your innovation and creativity, but rather the people around you. If you are a mover and shaker in-the-making, the people around you may feel threatened. If you start to put out 20 percent more product per week, stay one hour longer, or volunteer for that tough assignment, some coworkers will say, "What are you up to?" or "Are you apple polishing?" Movers and shakers as a rule remain uninhibited by these kinds of opinions. As you see and feel the resistance of coworkers, do not become defensive. Movers and shakers are risk-oriented people who shake off the negativism of others around them.

How Do You Know If You Are a Mover or Shaker?

If you are willing to encounter resistance and proceed with your plan, or if you intend to accelerate your career growth and get recognized for your achievements, first write down your goals. Then consider this key question: are you willing to follow your plan despite negative feedback, and will you exercise optimism and discipline to the degree necessary to meet your goals?

Will you start work an hour earlier and leave an hour later, take a training course, spend time with mentors and then mentor your junior associates? The extra effort might involve spending less time at lunch and not taking that afternoon coffee break, or volunteering for an assignment that scares you a little. Commit yourself to giving 110 percent; offering ideas, suggestions, and problem solutions; and improving your working relationship with those around you.

You don't have to be a workaholic; rather, pay attention to those things that will help to accelerate the progress you make toward your goals. Draw upon your discipline to be more productive during the time that you are at work.

Consider both the expressed and unexpressed needs of your boss, who may appreciate someone who makes an extra effort or who can operate without constant supervision.

Moving and Shaking in the Speaking Profession

Some forty years ago, while I was president of a conglomerate, I decided that when making corporate speeches I would always include music and mood lighting, and I would stand away from the lectern with a handheld microphone. Within my own companies I had no problem doing this because, of course, I was the boss who made thirty to forty speeches annually to the troops. However, as a by-product of the large consulting business we owned, I was giving about fifty or more paid speeches annually to other corporations and associations.

Once, I was booked by the regional VP of a national typewriter manufacturer for their national sales meeting. The date was confirmed by contract, and they paid a deposit. Approximately six weeks prior to the meeting, I was asked to stop by their headquarters in New York City to meet with the senior VP of sales.

We met. He told me of their final plans and briefly discussed my speaking style. He said, "Do I understand that you are going to have music at the beginning and the end, that you want to raise and lower the lights, and need a spotlight at the end?" I said, "Yes." Then he thanked me for the visit and I left. Subsequently he cancelled my speaking engagement. While this embarrassed the meeting planner and the regional VP who had booked me, it also disrupted my own schedule because I had already booked the date. However, I accepted the cancellation, kept the deposit, and did not invoke my contract or institute legal action.

The actions by this company caused me to ponder: people go to a movie and do not think anything about hearing music as the opening credits roll, attend a church service and automatically accept that organ music will be used to help lift spirits, or step on an elevator with soft music in the background and do not think twice about it. Yet, here was a company who didn't want music as part of stage dressing or speech support.

Throughout the ages, music has been used to create different moods and effects. Yet when I mentioned that my presentation included music, some meeting planners reacted as if I was introducing the plague.

I questioned whether or not I was on the right track because I knew I'd lose other bookings. Back then I hadn't seen anyone else use music or a change of lighting in a speech. This was my innovation; it felt right for me, and I knew of the positive impact on the audience when I had used it in the past. There were probably many times when I didn't even receive a call from a meeting planner because the idea of theatricality was so radically different from what many meeting planners perceived as good or great speaking.

As word of mouth regarding my presentation began to spread, I was booked more often. Among those who hired me, there was often significant resistance right up to the time that they could observe audience reaction, which was usually very favorable. Then the resistance began to melt away. Today my style of giving speeches and producing training videos with the use of music, varied lighting, different props, and theatrics is not only accepted but acclaimed.

Speaking to Speakers. Once, when I keynoted the annual convention of Toastmasters International in Washington, D.C., the audience included a gathering of delegates from forty countries and a total audience of over four thousand people. Many of the attendees made speeches as frequently as I did, so this was an audience that had heard everything and everybody concerning platform techniques.

My address was entitled "The EPOD Resolution" and was based upon the four dimensions—Energy, Persuasiveness, Optimism, and Discipline—to describe what makes some speeches more powerful, more moving, and ultimately remembered.

Although Toastmasters training teaches the use of a lectern and a prescribed introduction and closing technique, I held true to my style, including a presentation from center stage with a hand microphone, special lighting, and music. The fifty-five-minute speech was endorsed as one of the best that they had ever seen. Over ten thousand cassettes of the recorded presentation message sold within ninety days after this program and is still a popular recording marketed by many companies, including mine.

Toastmasters is an organization of movers and shakers. Toastmasters has over two hundred thousand members in ten thousand clubs and eighty countries. Many members are movers and shakers who use speaking as a powerful vehicle to enhance their career or business. Contact:

Toastmasters International
PO Box 9052
Mission Viejo, CA 92690 USA
Telephone: (949) 858–8255
Fax: (949) 858–1207
E-mail: tmembers@toastmasters.org
http:/www.toastmasters.org

No matter what you are trying to accomplish, maintain a firm belief in your ideas, bring the greatest amount of energy to them, and be willing to endure the indignities that may result. Movers and shakers stick with an idea or system longer than anyone else.

Risk and the Mover and Shaker

Large organizations do not tend to be risk-oriented. One looks at all the money that corporations pay to acquire a new division and regards this as a risk. But where is the risk? The big corporations mostly use shareholder money. If the new division fails, the corporation usually can recoup most of its investment. They will minimize their losses and spin it off.

In 1959, Ford produced the Edsel automobile, which quickly became a marketing disaster. It was considered one of the classic blunders in U.S. corporate history. Ford closed down the division and suffered a loss of hundreds of millions of dollars, including investments in advertising, machinery, tooling, parts, and related items. However, after they ceased manufacturing the Edsel, Ford still had the land, equipment, spare parts, and people—all transferable within the corporation. The inventory was quickly sold off. Their dealers were given other products to sell.

Examining the long-term dissolution of the Edsel division in light of the corporation's overall earnings reveals that it was not that much of a risk, yet the Ford Edsel is still seen as a high-risk, classic failure among corporations.

Risk orientation generally is more prevalent in medium to small-sized companies, and is the bailiwick of entrepreneurs and movers and shakers.

Movers and shakers are kin to entrepreneurs. Entrepreneurship involves developing a plan, adjusting it as needed, and proceeding. You don't give up on your plan because sales this quarter didn't meet expectations or because you couldn't anticipate all the variables. You can never anticipate all the variables.

> If you have a brand-new widget that isn't selling, then show it to more people, and somewhere, someone will buy it. A slice of the market will buy if exposed to what you are offering.

> When nine out of ten people say, "Not for me," a tenth person is out there who loves it. It may take extra effort to find him, but he is there.

Case #22: What You See . . . Is Not What You Get.

> "The real difference between most people is their degree of energy. A strong will and an invincible determination can accomplish almost anything. and therein lies the distinction between great and ordinary."
> —*Thomas Fuller*

A former marine, W. Mitchell, who once worked as a grip man on the San Francisco cable cars, cofounded a multimillion-dollar marketing company employing thousands, was twice elected mayor of a town in Colorado, ran for Congress, and had a career in radio and public television. This is the information that people like to hear about movers and shakers. He wrote a best-selling book, he has made hundreds of speeches, and he is a member of the Speaker's Hall of Fame. Yet the nexus of all these issues is the reality of W. Mitchell's life, an almost shocking story of the fates seemingly gone bad.

At age twenty-eight Mitchell's motorcycle collided with a truck, rendering him unconscious while causing gasoline to spread from the cycle's tank, which was ultimately ignited by a hot engine. This latter incident might have been fatal for most people. He suffered burns over 65 percent of his body. While his crash helmet had saved his scalp, most of his face and hands were literally burned off. His chances of survival were judged to be almost nil.

Months of work by skilled surgeons using the most modern techniques ultimately ended with a patchwork of grafted skin that later would cause a group of children in a schoolyard that he was passing to run away screaming, "Monster, monster."

In addition, his fingers and thumbs had been burned off completely and he was left with two stumps where his hands used to be and . . . the worst is yet to come.

Any human being suffering through such a horrendous accident would unquestionably go through bouts of depression and thoughts of throwing in the towel. As he rebuilt himself physically and emotionally, he decided to use his current condition as the basis from which he would grow. He moved to Colorado and became the mayor of a small town. He ran for Congress and built a sizeable business. He took flying lessons, acquired a commercial pilot's license, and bought a Cessna airplane.

On a morning in November, when the skies were clear and life was starting to look pretty good for Mitchell, this plane developed excessive icing on the wings at takeoff. At a height of one hundred feet the engine stalled. Within seconds it slammed into the runway, belly-up, bursting the fuel tank. He was conscious, and the dreaded thought of fire crossed his mind. However, he was removed from the aircraft and rushed to the hospital. Shortly thereafter, it was determined that this thirty-five-year-old man was paralyzed from the waist down and would be confined to a wheelchair for the rest of his life.

If you read his book or hear his recorded messages, all have a genesis of hope, inspiration, and positivity.

Having worked with him as a fellow speaker, I give personal testimony to the unbelievable energy and optimism that have become his imprimatur in everyday life as well as his professional speaking career.

How do you persuade others that goodness and personal growth can come from this tragedy? Mitchell's philosophy seems rather simplistic. He believes each of us has a choice. We can either decide that what has happened to us is so devastating that there is little point of moving forward, or we can adopt as a mantra, "It's not what happens to you in life that counts, it's what you do about it." In his speeches to corporations, schools, and hospitals he makes the following statement as the basis for his "game plan": "Before all of this happened to me, there were ten thousand things I could do. Now there are nine thousand. Sure, I could dwell on the one thousand that I can't do. But I prefer to think about the nine thousand that are left."

Undeniably, it takes W. Mitchell longer to perform the common tasks that you and I take for granted on a day-to-day basis. Completing a travel schedule that requires getting to the airport in advance, entering and departing an aircraft, and checking in and out of hotel rooms is complicated enough. In preparations for any speech, however, he requires that a small ramp be attached to the stage, allowing him to roll his wheelchair onto the stage without help. All of this requires a dedicated discipline to make it work daily. From his home in Santa Barbara, he travels to speaking engagements all over the world.

So we have examined his energy, optimism, and discipline. As to his skills of persuasion, the very manner in which he lives his life has unquestionably persuaded others that they too can be movers and shakers wherever they are.

The Testing Grounds of Innovation. Often, arguments about whether an innovation will work are made at a conference table. Meanwhile, the mover and shaker goes out and demonstrates that it does work, knowing that the way to find out if something will work is to test it in the field.

Simply because an idea doesn't initially appeal doesn't mean it won't work. With a twist here and a turn there it might be ready. Talk to twenty-five people a week for the next ten weeks to see if you have to modify and refine your idea.

The typical inventor of a new product thinks, *I know this will work. I have tested it in the lab and it has great application.* Then he takes it to manufacturers or distributors who say, "We don't see the value in it." Meeting this kind of resistance will cause the typical inventor to give up. If he or she is a mover and shaker, however, devotion to the idea sticks. Resistance and extended time horizons are a part of the process. They are emotionally prepared for the rocky road that awaits them.

It's worth repeating the statement I've had on my stationery for forty years:

> "The Power of Any Idea Can Be Measured by the Degree of Resistance It Attracts."

Case #203: Chicken Soup . . . Was Not Always Easy to Digest.

> "Success is creating a state of mind that allows you to achieve whatever it is you want."
>
> —*Mark Victor Hansen, coauthor,* Chicken Soup for the Soul

Time magazine, referring to the popular *Chicken Soup for the Soul* publications, said, "It is the publishing phenomena of the decade."

As of this writing, more than 82 million *Chicken Soup for the Soul* books have been sold in North America alone, and there are over one hundred licensed products in the United States. These accomplishments are a tribute to coauthors, Jack Canfield and Mark Victor Hansen. Although both men had independent success stories and had published numerous books and articles before, *Chicken Soup for the Soul* was not an easy sell or slam-dunk in the world of publishing. Thirty-seven rejection slips followed their submission of the original *Chicken Soup for the Soul* book.

Mark Victor Hansen, who incidentally wrote the introduction for this book, appears as an effervescent, exuberant, high-energy speaker in all of his public appearances; yet it is when he tells the story of the many setbacks in his life—filing for bankruptcy and the frequently rapid rejections of his book proposals—that he is at his best. The ability to be optimistic and remain disciplined are what obviously enabled him to sustain his energy and use his unquestionable persuasive powers.

A few years ago, Mark was honored with the prestigious Horatio Alger Award, which is given to American leaders who personify the virtues and principles inherent in the success stories written by nineteenth-century American author Horatio Alger. Mark Victor Hansen describes the most humbling moment of his life as the day he filed for bankruptcy, yet he concludes that at that moment he reinforced his desire to accomplish his dreams. He firmly believes, "If you want to live your dream, you need a dream to live."

I've had the good fortune to know and work with Mark for many years, mostly at times when he faced an uphill battle for recognition while facing what others might have concluded was failure. Instead each of his setbacks seem to increase his dedication. Through him I am reminded of an old bromide: "A person can fail many times, yet they are not a failure until they blame the circumstances on someone other than themselves."

Women in Management— Still the Untapped Resource

"If men are noted for courage, restlessness, and originality, then women are seen as nurturing, pleasing, and selfless. It is important not to downgrade the latter, since nurturing and kindness are as important as excellence in business."

[Author unknown]

Movers and shakers among women in management today are those who recognize that it is a risk-oriented world and there may be some nonsense to contend with along the way; still, the top is reachable.

I started my career in an era replete with nonsensical rules. For instance, in most companies you weren't considered for a management position unless you were the age of thirty. I suppose the prevailing wisdom was that you were not mature enough to be a manager until then. Fortunately, today we know this simply isn't true.

At that time minorities or those of a different ethnic, cultural, or racial heritage seldom became managers. Even into the 1990s, there was still bias and prejudice regarding women in top management positions. If a woman wanted to be a mover and shaker, she had to understand business was still mostly a male-dominated world. Frequently, women simply imitated male management styles to achieve their goals.

The majority of managers and business leaders are men, and the majority of business philosophies have been structured by men. This is not a value judgment about the situation; it simply is what it is. Women need opportunities in leadership positions before they can really restructure the male-dominated business world.

The woman who wants to succeed does not have to give up anything that she believes, but has to understand that to become a mover and shaker generally requires patience. During some presentations with executive women in the audience I write this statement up on the board:

A woman without her man is nothing.

Many women get upset with the statement. I ask why? It is the truest statement that has ever been made. Now as their ire climbs to a peak, I add two commas to the punctuation:

A woman, without her, man is nothing.

This exercise helps demonstrate that one has a choice: to find disfavor with what one perceives, or to consider new possibilities within the same apparent conditions. Women will continue to be a major force in business. As they reach the top, they have the opportunity to redefine old stereotypes and prove they are more than equal.

Happily we are seeing more and more women in sales organizations. At my seminars for sales organizations I used to see one or two women in a room of one hundred people. Now, among some groups, there are more women than men, and the sales leadership positions are frequently dominated by women. I recently did a program for a company that sold medical equipment, and four of the company's top twelve producers were women, including the top two.

EPOD Tactics

- Businesses that are efficient yet inhuman may succeed for a while—yet ultimately will fail.
- Every manager is a teacher. The measurement of his/her ability is the degree to which those who they manage learn.
- Instant success is usually a product of years of diligent effort marked by setbacks and failed enterprises.
- Mentors are always present in our lives. Yet, understanding how to use the information they offer and the behavior they exhibit is frequently difficult.
- Know when to let go of each other. Mentors and proteges often extend their relationship until they reach a point of diminishing return. They outgrow each other, and understanding this at the outset will help. It is dangerous when the mentor/protege relationship becomes one of dependency.
- You may have numerous mentors, though at the time you may not recognize them as such.
- Many problems exist in our society today. The people who are going to lead us to positive change will have the

courage of their conviction. It takes real guts to attempt new things. A powerful executive with courage takes risks and explores the unknown, however frightening it may be. Strong managers require the courage to shed old ideas and take risks with new ideas.
- Societies, like successful companies, are driven by ideas. The major movements created by Moses, Jesus, Buddha, and Mohammed were fueled by ideas. Each of these encountered resistance in the environments in which their ideas were first shared. It was their trial period, however, that created their following.
- Find a way in your company to encourage the sharing of ideas: suggestion boxes, staff meetings, internal memos. Then create an environment where the new ideas are welcomed, discussed, never ridiculed, and given a fair trial period.
- The front rows are vacant in meetings conducted with all males. Females, eager to be in the business world, fill up the front rows. Here is the genesis of moving and shaking.
- Women may represent the best untapped resource for companies who need new salespeople. As soon as management gets beyond its bias, it finds out how good they are.
- All things being equal, there is something about hearing a female voice answering the phone that makes callers feel better.
- To all would-be movers and shakers, I again extend the statement that was a mantra for every company I've ever run:

The Power of Any Idea Can Be Measured by the Degree of Resistance It Attracts.

CHAPTER 10
The Power of EPOD Speeches

In the Colosseum, a Roman guard responds to Caesar's query: "Why won't that lion eat the Christians?" The guard responds: "He's been told that after he's eaten he will be asked to say a few words."

The Book of Lists, published many years ago, described speaking to a group or audience as the greatest fear of most humans. Measure that statement against the level of importance that is attached to the skill of oral communication.

Every reader of this book has experienced speeches, some good, some bad, few of which are memorable.

The teacher, professor, religious advisor, corporate executive, politician, or seminar leader who was attempting to get and keep our attention and/or provide information which might possibly have a long-lasting effect often failed miserably.

Dr. Robert Cialdini, the author of *Influence: The Science and Practice* (Allyn & Bacon 4th Edition, 2001), summarizes his years of research in this statement:

> A lucky few have it; most of us do not. A handful of gifted "naturals" simply know how to capture an audience, sway the undecided, and convert the opposition. Watching these masters of persuasion work their magic is at once impressive and frustrating. What's impressive is not just the easy way they use charisma and eloquence to convince others to do as they ask.

It's also how eager those others are to do what is requested of them, as if the persuasion itself were a favor they couldn't wait to repay.

What makes a speech powerful, memorable, and exciting? Certainly preparation plays a major role, as does setting and circumstance. Timing can be a factor. Also consider the catchphrases used by President Franklin Roosevelt ("Americans have nothing to fear but fear itself"), Winston Churchill ("This will be their finest hour"), or Martin Luther King ("I have a dream").

While factors of **preparation, setting, circumstance,** and **timing** may be present in many speeches, few are considered powerful and even fewer are memorable. Abraham Lincoln, Theodore Roosevelt, Winston Churchill, Franklin Roosevelt, Dr. Martin Luther King, and Dr. Norman Vincent Peale have all made speeches that were classified as powerful and memorable; history has created a niche for their words.

The research used in **Power Linguistics** leads to the conclusion that a powerful and memorable speech contains the four dimensions of EPOD which, when effected by the speaker, leave a lasting, remembered impression on the audience. These four dimensions are all inexorably tied to each other: Energy (E), Persuasion (P), Optimism (O), and Discipline (D).

Energy

In speaking, high levels of energy have little to do with the age, sex, or athletic prowess of the speaker.

Dr. Norman Vincent Peale, at age ninety, demonstrated an energy level that could have run a generator. Dr. Ruth Westheimer generated as much energy as a male twice her size, and President Franklin Roosevelt, despite being bound to braces, crutches, and wheelchairs throughout most of his adult life, emanated a level of energy in his speeches that unquestionably lifted the spirit and optimism of a nation experiencing economic depression and ultimately the greatest war in modern history.

Your energy package will be perceived by audiences based on your enthusiasm, projection, eye contact, voice level, and gestures as well as its connection to content. Don't confuse the audience by simply raising your voice, yelling, or speaking bombastically. On the contrary, energy is created internally. It mostly comes from the way you feel about yourself and the audience.

Much of your energy level is determined before you speak. Have you done your research and preparation? Then don't waste energy through hyper-nervousness. If your speech is prepared properly, you know your audience and have checked out the environment in which the speech will be made (lighting, sound system, staging); then it is time to direct your energies internally. Relax and observe your audience. Enjoy the moment and absorb what's going on. The audience measures your energy level by the degree of excitement and enthusiasm you attach to your words. Your gestures and overall body stance on the podium and at the lectern reinforce their perceptions.

If you're working from notes, highlight or underline key words and phrases to ensure that you emphasize them during the delivery. Many great speakers indicate in the margin of their prepared notes where they wish to use a dramatic gesture. Rehearsing the speech with prepared notes allows the energy to flow naturally and prevents mechanical or overly theatrical delivery.

A number of years ago, John Bremner, author of a handbook on the use of words, wrote about speakers. He said, "In the United States, where two or three are gathered together, there is a guest speaker. This tribal ritual starts with a speaker, who introduces a speaker, who introduces the guest speaker, who introduces his speech with some weighty words such as, 'It is indeed a pleasure and a privilege for me to be with you here today, and I certainly want to thank Mr. Babbitt for inviting me, and Mr. Blabalot for introducing me.'"

The few who are still listening are then invited to "share a funny story the speaker was reminded of as he was coming here today." The story has already lost whatever punch it might have had, because the guest speaker has announced that what he is about to say is a story, and a funny one at that.

When the story ends, the guest speaker condescendingly signals a change of tone with the somber line, "Seriously, however

. . ." He probably has lost his audience, or deserves to have. Bremner describes the failings of those speakers who lacked a true understanding of the technique required. He said, "They waste precious moments of an opening by uttering banalities, thus diminishing the energy. They tell listeners that they are going to tell them something, and worse, they attempt to telegraph moods rather than build the energy which allows the listener to decide what is interesting, funny, or serious."

The payoff for extensive preparatory work is when the audience senses your energy and responds with applause or other kudos. High energy begets high energy.

Persuasion

The art of persuasion is a complicated process, based more on perception than reality. The eminent writer Oscar Wilde once said, "The value of an idea has little to do with the sincerity of the person who expresses it."

The most valuable ideas frequently fall on deaf ears because the speaker's level of persuasion is so low that the audience perceives the idea as lacking validity. Many speakers simply lack conviction and sincerity when presenting their ideas.

One of the most powerful speakers in the twentieth century was Adolf Hitler. While I do not support or condone his evil tactics, objectively assessing his speaking capability, he had a powerful technique for spell-binding audiences, while leading his nation into disaster.

When he spoke to groups of people, he would look for indications of resistance. When he discerned resistance or disagreement, he would hit his audience with one idea after another in rapid fire. Then he would heighten the emotional tone of his presentation to subdue resistance.

Often he would make his speeches at night using floodlights and torches for dramatic impact. He raised his presentations to a fever pitch with his onlookers screaming for more. He turned his language into an emotional fountain.

The basic tool at Hitler's disposal was his ability to express himself and his use of language. He wasn't physically endowed.

He wasn't a great warrior, celebrated general, or someone known for high intellect. Despite his evil intent, one can learn much from his style of persuasion.

Individuals who have high skill levels but don't possess the ability to speak face roadblocks throughout their careers. Many dwell in obscurity.

Why? Because they don't work on their language capability and harness the power of speech.

The first condition of a persuasive speech is to know the audience: what they do, the issues they're dealing with, and what brings them together. The persuasive speech is delivered at the audience's level of perception and tailored explicitly for them. Use analogies, metaphors, or statistics that relate to their work, background, and level of sophistication. Remember: it's about them, not you.

Persuasive speeches contain words and phrases selected to create feelings of well-being in the audience. A simple rule of thumb is to reduce the number of first-party references (*I, we, me*) and increase the number of second- and third-party references (*you, your, yours; they, them*).

Try to eliminate value-judging phrases. Words such as *should, ought,* and *must* create a distinct psychological resistance from the listener. Instead of telling people what they have to do, what they haven't done, and what they need to do, cite examples that they can identify with, understand, and follow. Political speeches are notorious for the use of derogatory and sometimes vilifying comments. This may elicit an immediate audience response, but in the long run, negativity reduces the effectiveness of the speech.

A persuasive message speaks to the heart. It says, "I understand you. I know where you're coming from. I can almost feel your pain. I empathize with you. Here is our common bond; I give you this idea which I hope will be of help."

Case #107: Who Will Remember Your Address?

"The world will little note nor long remember what we say here."

—Abraham Lincoln, "Gettysburg Address"

Examine the circumstances and structure of one of the most powerful and remembered speeches in American history.

In September 1863 a committee was formed to create a dedication service for a new military cemetery in Gettysburg, Pennsylvania. They decided to invite the man considered as one of the greatest living orators in the United States to speak at the ceremony.

The town was the site of one of the most devastating battles in world history. Fifty thousand men died over the few days of this conflict, part of a civil war that would eventually take more than 620,000 lives.

The committee planned the ceremony for October 1863, and in case you believe you know who the speaker was and what the speech was about, the following information may be a revelation.

The speaker selected was Dr. Edward Everett, the president of Harvard University. Common to the times, he was asked to speak for two hours, a normality in an age before radio, television, or movies. Dr. Everett agreed to speak, yet asked that he be given until November to prepare. His style included impeccable preparation, for he was to cite accurate dates, times, heroes, calamities, and other emotional issues of the war.

Dr. Everett's speech would be written, studied, corrected, and memorized. It would take approximately two hours and fifteen minutes to deliver, and ultimately the audience was moved, inspired, and awed.

However, between Dr. Everett's agreement to come to Gettysburg and the actual event, many dignitaries were invited: governors, other city and state leaders, active and retired military officers, and, as an afterthought, President Abraham Lincoln. The invitees theorized he could come, make a few remarks, and depart on the same day because of Gettysburg's proximity to Washington.

The truth is that Lincoln arrived the night before. To shatter another myth, his remarks were not jotted on the back of the envelope. He had in the thirty days allotted progressively developed four versions of his address. He delivered the final version. It contained ten sentences—272 words—and was constructed in a form known as the Hellenic tradition. The first portion of the speech was dedicated to *epainesis* (extolling the dead), while the second portion followed the form of *parainesis* (exhorting the living). The whole presentation lasted a little over three minutes, yet it has endured as a memorable presentation for almost a century and a half.

It is not revisionist history to point out that Lincoln's early life was in a rough-hewn culture and that much of what he knew was self-taught. Through discipline and study he mastered the technique of speech development. His Gettysburg Address was made as an aftermath of Dr. Everett's well-received oration, timely remarks made by other dignitaries, a most thoughtful benediction, and soul-stirring music by a choir. Observe the first stanza of Lincoln's address:

> Four score and seven years ago our forefathers brought forth on this continent a new nation, conceived in liberty and dedicated to the proposition that all men are created equal.

He sent energy to his listeners. Observe that the only first-person reference is "our forefathers" (a collective noun connecting him with the listener and other citizens).

The avoidance of first-person language (*I, we, me*) or aggrandizements of his position ("as your president" or "as commander in chief") sends a combination of energy and persuasion to the listener. Again, it's about them, not him or his political party or accomplishments.

Now observe the second stanza:

> Now we are engaged in a great civil war, testing whether that nation or any nation so conceived and so dedicated can long endure.

There are no attempts at political correctness or justification for his actions, no condemnations of the Confederacy, no requests for retribution or punishment. Again, the energy and persuasion touches the feelings of the listener.

In the next stanza we hear purpose:

> We are met on a great battlefield of that war. We have come to dedicate a portion of that field as a final resting-place for those who here gave their lives that that nation might live. It is altogether fitting and proper that we should do this. But in a larger sense, we cannot dedicate, we cannot consecrate, we cannot hallow this ground. The brave men, living and dead, who struggled here have consecrated it far above our poor power to add or detract.

There is no reference to winners or losers. He glorifies the brave men who are being interred, both Union and Confederate (*epainesis*). Again he does not ask for retribution or punishment.

In the next stanza he starts his optimistic appeal to the listener's heart:

> The world will little note nor long remember what we say here, but it can never forget what they did here. It is for us the living rather to be dedicated here to the unfinished work which they who fought here have thus far so nobly advanced.

Notice the repeated use of the word "dedicate" and the implication that all participants nobly advanced. It is in the second part of this stanza that Lincoln moves into *parainesis*.

In the final stanza he repeats the use of "dedication" and asks in conclusion for their optimism and discipline.

> It is rather for us to be here dedicated to the great task remaining before us—that from these honored dead we take increased devotion to that cause for which they gave the last full measure of devotion—that we here highly resolve that these dead shall not have died in vain, that this nation under God shall have a new birth of freedom.

Observe again the use of the words "us" and "we." Again these first-person narratives are collectives identifying the living and the dead of both the North and South as having had a common goal, to restructure the Union. He ends with an optimistic and persuasive appeal to all those present and to all those who will later read his words.

> And that government of the people, by the people, for the people shall not perish from the earth.

Despite the greatness of Lincoln's address, the crowd stood in shock. It was over so quickly, and what had they heard? Some members of the press in reporting to their papers said, "The buffoon did it again."

This remarkable speech is a treatise to the power of EPOD-style speaking. Its brevity, thoughtful compilation, and magnificent enduring quality are truly a benchmark for those who wish to achieve powerful, positive outcomes from their communication.

Optimism in Speaking

How do you begin to sell optimism in a negative world? Examine the front page of your local newspaper or listen to the television or radio newscaster, and you'll note that most issues and stories are presented in a negative manner. Television interviews are conducted using negative questions or statements that ask us to see the downside of almost everything.

In a world filled with negativity, you as a speaker, presenter, teacher, or spiritual leader have the option of following the crowd or selling the positive elements of virtually any set of circumstances. A speaker has an ideal opportunity to radiate positivity and present the optimistic side of issues that most people do not think to examine on their own. "Is the bottle half full or half empty?" "Is 7 percent unemployment really 93 percent employment?" These examples are triggering devices. Certainly it is wise to beware of calamities or dangerous conditions; however, most people are interested in solutions. They want to hear thoughts and ideas that explain how to deal with these critical or negative situations.

If you are speaking to an audience which recently had to deal with rapid changes or adverse circumstances, cite encouraging case histories of those who have victoriously dealt with similar situations.

Optimism also means telling people they "can." It means taking facts and presenting them so that the audience can discern an immediate advantage. Many years ago, I heard a professor say, "Statistics are like bikinis; what they reveal is interesting, what they conceal is vital." Thus, issues such as surveys, statistics, and similar data are best received when presented as positives.

An optimistic presentation requires preparation prior to speaking. Avoid things that tend to bring pessimism to your surroundings or your own psyche. Avoid reading the front page of the newspaper or listening to negative issues presented by the media, or take the statements from these sources and create a diametrically opposed position. Your audience will love it. Occasionally, you may get criticism based on a lack of fact-finding research. Just remember, the news sources do the same thing.

Have you ever noticed that most speakers attempt to use humor as a means to create synergy between themselves and their audience? The late Bill Gove, a phenomenal speaker and storyteller, used to say, "It's difficult to be depressed when you're smiling." He also lamented that great leaders often had poor writers.

A well-delivered line, such as those credited to past presidents Roosevelt, Reagan, and Clinton, or Prime Minister Churchill, had its origin in the mind of the speechwriter who carefully researched potential listeners and critics.

Case #266: Humor Me, Please.

"Life does not cease to be funny when someone dies, any more than it ceases to be serious when someone laughs."

—*George Bernard Shaw*

One of the best humorists I have ever heard speak was Charles W. Jarvis, a dentist from San Marcos, Texas. His timing, execution, facial contortion, and body language were without peer.

The funny thing about funny people is that they are frequently intellectuals, serious professionals, or even products of tragedy. A favored expression of Dr. Jarvis is, "Humor is a painful thing told playfully."

Robert Orben was frequently called "the funniest man in politics," a title earned writing for Barry Goldwater and other political aspirants, and eventually becoming chief speech writer for President Gerald R. Ford and then director of the White House speechwriting staff. His close friends call him "the prince of optimism."

Bob is the author of forty-seven books. He sharpened his skills in the comedic arena as a writer for comedians Dick Gregory, Jack Paar, Red Skelton, and others.

Now examine some reality. Born in the Bronx borough of New York City in 1927, he grew up during the height of the Depression, living with his parents and brother in a one-bedroom walk-up flat. Ironically, the $21 a month rent had to be traded for a $9 a month apartment if the family were to continue to have a roof over their head. There were few jobs available, and both his father and older brother faced many bleak tomorrows knowing that unemployment was always threatening. As Bob tells it, poverty is frequently the birthplace of ingenuity. So with optimism in hand and with the persuasion of Walter, his twenty-seven-year-old brother, Bob Orben, then thirteen years old, worked the Catskills, the font of apprenticeship for many comedians. He appeared as: "The boy with the radio mind," a mentalist, with his brother the Svengali master-minding the act. They passed the hat and whatever they received became a help to the distressed family.

Along the way, Bob recites, "You had to be optimistic. We would go from place to place, do our half-hour mental act with the most obvious of codes, and then pass the hat. It kept us alive for the summer." He was also quick to add, "We didn't represent a threat to any established mentalists on the circuit." When he graduated from Theodore Roosevelt

High School and recognized there would be no college, he optimistically worked with what he had to become, as one editor called him, "the funniest man in politics."

Again, reality loomed. To fulfill a goal of twenty-five jokes a day, seven days a week, he rose each day at 5:30 and proceeded to imbibe two or three cups of hot coffee and read the daily newspapers and available magazines to look for the things and issues that he could turn into "funny."

Think about it. You produce thirty to fifty jokes for one client, and perhaps five to seven of those make it out of the starting block. Your discipline feeds your energy, your energy produces product, and then you turn it over to someone who you hope will use the product well.

Bob Orben emphasizes that comedy and speechwriting became his way of life. He looked at every incident and occurrence in his daily activity as having potential for creating a "funny" thing. Once, when undergoing minor surgery, as he came out from under the anesthesia, he kept saying the word, "pencil." The attending nurse out of both curiosity and concern stood by and asked what he needed. When the word "pencil" was repeated again two or three times, he was brought a writing pad and pencil, and the nurse soon learned that he wanted to write a joke that had just come to him as he moved from the haze of anesthesia to full awakedness.

Bob followed ten basic rules by which he would operate as a comedy writer and then went on to point out it wasn't the rules alone, it was the discipline to adhere to the rules that made the difference.

1. Use topical material.
2. Think before you speak.
3. Recognize the difference between wit and comedy.
4. Don't necessarily mix comedy styles.
5. Keep your interest in learning alive.
6. Be clever or funny in all that you do.
7. Gags and grammar don't mix.

8. Discover what you really look and sound like.
9. Keep your eyes, ears and notebook open.
10. Get something new.

When asked to assess the difference in the level of pressure when writing comedy for television versus writing comedy for the White House, Bob responds, "Two things I remember most about the White House are the tension and the need to deliver on a much higher level. Writing for television is a high-pressure way to make a living, but if a comic monologue goes bad, the damage is limited. When you write for the president of the United States, if you make a mistake it's on the evening news. *That's pressure.*"

Now imagine: should you ever contemplate a similar career, beyond the need for a clear understanding of how the listener will think and feel, it is necessary to draft the material that fits the persona of the person who will speak the material, as well as the audience. If the material doesn't always work, you will be the first to know, and if it works well, the listener may not understand the joke writer's participation.

You can also use affirmations as a principle for creating optimistic feelings. I tell audiences that optimism is mostly a choice, and that every morning before I speak I make a choice. Each morning when you face the mirror to shave or put on makeup, you have an opportunity to sell optimism to that audience of one. Personally, I choose to affirm myself each day by reciting out loud to my mirror image.

> "I am a unique and precious being, created by God for very special purposes. I'm doing the very best I can. I'm ever growing in love and awareness. This day is mine. No one can take it away from me."

This and other parts of my affirmation set the stage for my optimism, and I attempt to radiate that as I speak.

I'm also reminded of the words of St. Francis of Assisi: "Lord, make me an instrument of thy peace. Where there is despair, let me sow hope." The degree of optimism in your speech raises the audience's level of hope and gives them a desire to identify with and participate in your message.

Discipline

The discipline level of a speaker may not be apparent to the audience. However, the results of the speaker's discipline before and during a speech are what can make the speech powerful and memorable.

Discipline starts with preparation. Do you know what you're going to say? Have you done your research? Have you put it in a format (notes or otherwise) to retrieve and deliver? Have you practiced your timing, inflections, and nuances?

The fact is that when a speech begins and ends on time, it's because the speaker has exercised discipline regarding the audience, other speakers, and the meeting planner.

Great speakers end their speeches on time. I've seen hundreds of professionals exceed their time allotments, stray from their subject matters, and break some of the simplest rules of powerful speaking. Why do they fail to see that anything that can upset the program or the audience is distracting?

A speaker's discipline frequently begins with a personal commitment. If your speeches are to be powerful and memorable, you have to be in the physical and mental shape to deliver. Any excess prior to a speech—such as overeating, imbibing, or late-night reveling—will reduce your effectiveness.

As someone who has made over five thousand speeches, I have frequently been invited to cocktail parties and celebrations the night before the event at which I'm scheduled to speak. I always accept, yet hold my intake to nonalcoholic beverages. I have seen many speakers accept these invitations, then imbibe, thinking the wages of dissipation will dissipate tomorrow. Unfortunately, that's rarely the case.

You can only deliver a high level of energy when you feel energetic, and you can only be persuasive and optimistic when you look and act that way. Discipline means knowing when to say no.

To emphasize the importance of discipline, I frequently share a portion of my personal history. I entered speech therapy in the Philadelphia school system at the age of six, and for seven years I was tutored in the basics of sound fundamental speech. Because of a congenital problem, I didn't speak correctly when I entered the system, so the therapists hammered home the exercises and practice pieces that I had to work on constantly. I don't believe I became a professional speaker by coincidence, but rather by disciplined training.

I frequently wonder why those who are familiar with the rules of sound preparation for speaking don't follow them. Thus, only a small percentage emerge as powerful and memorable speakers. My conclusion is: to know and not to do is not to know.

The EPOD Theory is based on my observations and experiences in making more than five thousand speeches, but more importantly, in dealing with more than five thousand audiences. A good speaker, like the conductor of a giant orchestra, will lead the audience from one emotional state to another. The Churchills, Roosevelts, and Martin Luther Kings of the world consciously formed a methodology which, when emulated, lent energy, persuasiveness, and optimism to their delivery. Discipline is a matter of commitment, the level of which only you can determine. If all elements are in balance, the audience is rewarded.

EPOD Tactics

- The real measurement of your speaking ability is: can they and will they understand what you have said?
- Confucius said:

  "If language is not correct then what is said . . . is not what is meant;
  If what is said is not meant, then what has to be done remains undone;
  If this remains undone morals and art will deteriorate;
  If morals and art deteriorate, justice will go astray;

If justice goes astray, the people will stand about in helpless confusion."

- Visualize the tremendous cauldron of energy inside you which drives the human body. Imagine this energy converted into your projection, your gestures, and your dynamic flow of words. The audience measures your energy level by the degree of excitement and enthusiasm you attach to your words. Your gestures and overall body stance at the lectern reinforce their perception.
- If an incident has occurred in the last thirty to sixty days, or, even a few hours before your speech, tailor your remarks so that the audience hears them as specifically for them.
- Great speakers and their speeches can be measured on three levels:

    Ethos: Getting to the value system of your listeners.
    Logos: Is there a logical progression that people can follow? As long as they listen they need to be able to identify with what is going on.
    Pathos: Injecting into the speech that part of your life that is probably painful.

- If the speaker's life history or experience serves as an example, the audience identifies with the issue and the growth. Most great speakers have a fair amount of disclosure in their presentations.
- The proper use of language becomes a symphony for the ear.
- If you are speaking to an audience that is dealing with rapid change, poor results, or adverse circumstances, cite case histories of those who have gained victory over insurmountable odds while encountering similar challenges.
- When a speech begins and ends on time, it's because the speaker has exercised concern and discipline regarding the audience, other speakers, and the meeting planner.
- Individuals who have high skill levels but who don't possess the ability to speak face roadblocks throughout their careers.

- Audiences typically are moving through a variety of emotional states. If they have not heard you speak before, the first stage is apprehension. If you are provocative, they may become agitated or irritated. If your message is dull or low energy, that will be their response as well. When you redefine the provocative issue, their own insights make them comfortable. A great speech delivered by an effective speaker leaves the audience wishing for more. Think of it as four emotional states: **scared, mad, glad, sad**.
- Avoid cursing, obscenities, and scatological language. These forms of expression may have their place; however, the platform, screen, or public gatherings are not that place. If you wish to be persuasive, remember:

    Hell is a place, damned is a curse; certain four-letter words are obscene, and references to waste matter are scatological. To use them outside of their context connotes a lack of intelligence or limited vocabulary.

CHAPTER 11

Effective Communication

"The modern method of instruction has not yet strangled the holy curiosity of inquiry. It is a grave error to believe that the enjoyment of seeing and searching can be promoted by means of coercion and sense of duty."

—*Albert Einstein*

By the time you were six years old you had probably developed many of the speech patterns that you use today. How you say something, your grammar, the context in which you say it, your syntax, and the cliches you use most often were mostly acquired in your formative years. Yes, you learn the rules of grammar through formal education, yet the basic way in which you use language is usually established before you attend high school.

Today, even those with sophisticated educations have extensive flaws in their speech and writing habits. Some of the errors are harmless, particularly if used in purely social conversation. However, in the world of business or education, miscommunication often generates an outcome that was not intended.

If your communication has a distinct purpose and desired outcome, then it is important to consider how what you are attempting to communicate is being received. In short, will the listener or reader of your communication understand what you are trying to say? Then, will they act on your words, appropriate to your intention?

The modern dictionary contains approximately 550,000 words, while the average individual uses only 2 or 3 percent of those available. How many words do you use, and what are you doing to expand your vocabulary?

Complicating this mix of information is an exposure force that continues to influence the communication style of most people. In this new millennium, we are bombarded daily with written and spoken communications of all kinds of styles. We experience the repetition of many phrases to the extent that we adopt them as our own cliches.

Examine the overuse of the word "like" as if it were a form of punctuation, or the word "okay" as a pause or seemingly asking for approval.

Politicians respond to important questions with the phrase: "To be honest with you . . . ," or "To tell the truth . . . ," unconsciously implying that many of their responses may not be honest or truthful. Managers use coercion, intimidation, and implied threats as pseudo motivation. Teachers, seminar leaders, salespeople, and others who profess high-level communication skills ask the question, "Do you follow me?" after proffering an idea, without realizing the listener's brain transmits this as, "I [the speaker] am smart, you [the listener] are not as smart, so listen better."

The measure of all communication is the outcome achieved. If you are not getting the outcomes you desire from your communications, the solution is to change what you are doing.

Start by examining the number of cliches that have infiltrated your speech. Take our **Power Linguistics** cliche test, which follows. Then you may wish to find other means of expression to improve your communications.

The Cliche

A cliche is a phrase or expression to spice up what might otherwise appear dull, frequently used to make or emphasize a particular issue within the communication. Research indicates when these are used the majority of listeners/readers "tune out" momentarily and may miss or misinterpret a portion of the message which follows.

Here is a partial list of those cliche (phrases) which have come into more than common use:

Your personal evaluation of use

	Seldom	Freq.	Not at all
At the end of the day	___	___	___
In the long run	___	___	___
The use of "like" as if it were a form of puncuation	___	___	___
Twenty four, seven	___	___	___
Around (in place of about)	___	___	___
Without a doubt	___	___	___
Awesome	___	___	___
May I help you?	___	___	___
Ballpark figure	___	___	___
On a weekly basis—vs—weekly	___	___	___
Between a rock and a hard place	___	___	___
Bottom line	___	___	___
It's not rocket science	___	___	___
Literally, as a precedent to an observation or suggestion	___	___	___
Pushing the envelope	___	___	___
Thinking outside the box	___	___	___
To be honest with you, to be perfectly honest, to tell the truth	___	___	___
Touch bases	___	___	___
The word "okay" as a pause or asking for approval	___	___	___
Do you follow me?	___	___	___

Next, examine some common words or phrases which you may have used to make or stress a point. Then ponder the confusion that arises when these words or phrases are directed toward a listener raised in another culture.

- Boxing rings are square, automobiles are rated by horsepower, mobile homes are stationary, and we seldom rest in a restaurant.
- The extension of flammable is inflammable. Yet, they both mean the same thing.
- English muffins are American, hamburgers don't contain ham, and the hotdog has no connection to the canine family.
- There is no egg in eggplant, no pine in pineapple, no grape in grapefruit.
- Most Frenchmen had never heard of French fries until they were introduced to them by the Americans, and our Venetian blinds were invented in China.
- We make appointments with friends, yet, if romance is involved, it's a date, and if it doesn't work out, we don't give a fig.
- We refer to a runny nose, butter fingers, and being bug-eyed.
- We speak of things that burn up or houses that burn down as if they had a direction of choice.
- We ask people to deplane, implying that the plane will be lifted from us, and we run over to see someone who may be run down.

Now examine these sentences where a word spelled the same means otherwise within the same sentence:

- The bandage was wound around the wound.
- The farm was used to produce produce.
- The dump was so full that it had to refuse more refuse.
- He could lead if he could get the lead out.
- The soldier decided to desert his dessert in the desert.
- Since there is no time like the present, he thought it was time to present the present.

- The dove dove into the bushes.
- I did not object to the object.
- The insurance was invalid for the invalid.
- There was a row among the oarsmen about how to row.
- The buck does funny things when the does are present.
- The wind was too strong to wind in the sail.
- After a number of injections my jaw got number.
- Upon seeing the tear in the painting I shed a tear.
- I had to subject the subject to a series of tests.

If your desire is to improve the outcome of your communications, examine a few of the easier-to-adapt formats that grew out of our seventeen-year study.

Affirming Language

Affirming language has a positive impact on almost everyone. Surprisingly, affirming language is in contrast to most management language; it excludes value-judging phrases such as *you should, you ought, you must*. Often, affirming language is mistaken as praise. The difference between affirming language and praise is subtle. Affirming language affirms the individual for what they are, and praise usually contains a condition or "hook." Examine the following examples:

PRAISE: I love you when you [get good grades] [cooperate] [meet your goals].

AFFIRMATION: I appreciate the effort you put into your . . .

PRAISE: I admire you when you get your paperwork done on time.

AFFIRMATION: The way you complete your paperwork on time really helps the whole department. Thank you!

If I affirm you and acknowledge the effort that you have made, you will usually want the affirmation again. Most people are not affirmed nearly enough, and many have not been affirmed in years. Humans want to be affirmed because it leaves them with a good feeling and raises their feelings of self-worth.

> When we receive affirming language, we do not perceive ourselves as good or bad, right or wrong, **but simply worthy.**

You may ask why the use of "worthy" and its counterpart "unworthy" are not a form of value judging. The answer is as follows:

> When your self-esteem is high you feel worthy, and when your self-esteem is low you feel unworthy. However, you are **always** worthy, independent of how you may feel.

There is no value attached to that latter statement. Suppose a worker produces eight units per hour, yet the average worker does ten. Is the first worker any less worthy as an individual? Of course not. He might not have worked as diligently as he could, yet he is no less worthy. He is still the same person.

When we tell an employee that we appreciate his or her effort, we are separating the effort from the employee. When we say, "You did very well," there is no separation of worker and effort. None of this precludes creating methods by which the worker can expand their production.

Remember, we are examining the effect of communication on the listener. While the difference between praise and affirmation seems subtle or even a matter of semantics, the prevailing wisdom is that praise can be detrimental.

Alice Miller, a world-renowned psychologist and researcher, researched the effects of praise and affirmation on the psyche of children in her book entitled *Prisoners of Childhood* (Basic Books, Inc., 1981). She relates the following:

> It is one of the turning points in analysis when a disturbed patient comes to the emotional insight that all the love that he has captured with so much effort and self-denial was not meant for him as he really was, that the admiration for his beauty and

achievements was aimed at this beauty and these achievements, and not at the child himself.

In analysis, the small and lonely child who has hidden behind his achievements wakes up and asks, "What would have happened if I would have appeared before you bad, ugly, angry, jealous, lazy, dirty, smelly? Where would your love have been then?

And was I all these things as well? Does this mean that it was not really me whom you loved but only what I pretended to be? The well-behaved, reliable, empathetic, understanding and convenient child who in fact was never a child at all.

I cite this excerpt not to condemn those who use praise, but rather to ask them to find ways to convert their praise into affirmation so as to get more positive outcomes.

Affirmations aid in the development of rapport and are extremely effective in new situations. Imagine a new customer calling a place of business.

If your telephone is currently answered as follows, "Good morning, XYZ Corporation, Betty speaking," script the receptionist to say, "Thank you for calling XYZ Corporation. How may I direct your call?"

In this example the caller is thanked, mentioned first, and affirmed—all elements of **Power Linguistics**. Try this simple experiment with your phone response and measure the effect. If you are addressing a group, irrespective of their size or importance, start out with, "Thank you for the opportunity to be with you today."

A salesperson meeting a prospect for the first time usually whips out his business card, introduces himself and his company, and maybe even refers to the product or service—all before any reference to the prospect.

If you are a salesperson or trainer, try one of these affirming exercises:

- "Mr. Jones, thank you for the opportunity to spend a few minutes explaining the purpose of my call."
- "Mr. Jones, your time is important, so thank you for the opportunity."

Note the simplicity of the change. The customer's name is first; they are thanked and affirmed for their decision to grant you an interview.

In their early use, you will experience some discomfort; so remember, it takes twenty-one days to change even the simplest behavior, and in the early stages you are experiencing what we call "a response to your awkward stage." Once you get past this stage, the new language will become routine.

An affirming statement validates a person or an assertion. It can be a positive declaration that ratifies a decision, such as, "I affirm your wise choice." Affirmations are introduced in the early stages of a relationship, and the same affirmation, as well as others, are repeated frequently to sustain the feelings of well-being in those who have been affirmed.

Affirmations are frequently completed with limited or no dialogue, such as when the other party is making a point. The listener responds with frequent nods and smiles.

Incidentally, the simplest and most rewarding way to practice affirmations is to create your own, for yourself.

Does the latter sound confusing? When I first wrote *How to Have a Good Year Every Year* (Berkley Press, 1991), I referred to my personal affirmation written by me, for me, and recited by me, to me daily. We received more letters and calls about this portion of the book than any other.

Here it is. Repeated daily it is a personal wake-up call to positivity, and my reminder to affirm others early and often:

> I am a unique and precious being—created by God for very special purposes. I am ever doing the best I can. I am ever growing in love and awareness. This day is mine. No one can take it away from me.

You see how this affirms me. However, as I said, it is also my daily reminder to affirm others.

The Good, the Bad, and the Ugly

The words "bad," "dumb," "stupid," and "ugly" are but a few of the ill-chosen selections people use to describe others whose actions are undesirable in their sight. To imply that they are essentially demotivators is an understatement.

Put-down statements, pejoratives, and most name calling come under the heading of value judging, a language style that is demeaning and nonproductive, usually taking energy from both sides of the communication.

Think about it: most people don't do things intentionally to create negative outcomes, do they? Your employees or your boss doesn't say or do things to intentionally make you feel bad. Would it be worth practicing a new style of language to attempt to offset these negative circumstances?

When someone makes a mistake in judgment and the outcome is a costly error or unpleasant circumstance, it will be difficult to remember that at the time the decision was made, the individual probably thought he/she was doing the right thing. The rationalization is that if they had known how to do better, they would have done so. We could then correctly label the outcome as an outgrowth of a wise or unwise decision.

You may think to yourself: "Aren't the use of 'wise' and 'unwise' value judging?"

The answer is: the use of "unwise" here is an after-the-fact observation. If you felt it important to be on time and alert for your meeting, and you are horribly hung over, it is appropriate and not value judging to observe that you made an unwise decision the night before.

If you speak loudly in the library when everyone is trying to read, that is neither good or bad; it is inappropriate. The library is traditionally not the place to raise your voice. If you attend a football game and you yell, that may be appropriate.

Value Judging Is Detrimental in Business. Suppose you and I have a buy/sell relationship. Through language, if we value judge each other, we are ultimately going to experience a breakdown in the relationship. Suppose you are the customer and are calling my company because you did not receive the service that you wanted. If my customer service representative value judges your language, he will not be effectively serving you, maintaining your business, and fulfilling the responsibilities of his job.

> In business, if you place your value system over mine, then you will judge me, which will lead to a detriment in our relationship.

Suppose you raise your voice over the phone, and the service rep responds by saying, "Sir, would you please lower your voice? You are shouting in my ear." Your response may be, "You bet I'm shouting." By reprimanding you, the service rep has value judged you and is going to gain nothing.

Instead, by saying, "Sir, I can tell you are very upset," he/she has acknowledged your behavior. You respond, "Oh, you can tell I'm upset, huh? How can you tell?" The service rep continues, "I can tell, sir, and I regret anything that we've done that has made you this upset." By using this type of language he/she will be able to more quickly and more effectively handle the customer's grievance, while increasing the probability of retaining the customer.

> The language that an effective customer service representative uses is not something that comes naturally. In most cases it has to be taught.

Raised in a society that makes value judgments about virtually every aspect of life, people do not tend to use affirming language even when it would be in their best interest to do so.

Nordstrom's, Wal-Mart, and similar organizations train their people to use affirming language because they understand the results that it produces. Language is important in preserving relationships. The feeling you have following an encounter with a store salesperson, particularly how you feel at the end of the encounter, profoundly affects your feelings towards the company.

Here we have excerpted from our **Power Linguistic** program some commonly used phrases and the options that we teach:

Conventional Phrase	Options
Should, as in:	
You should—	Need to—
You should have—	Could have considered—
They should—	Have options such as—
Ought, as in:	
You ought to—	Might want to—
Everyone ought to have—	May desire to—
They ought to—	Can consider—
Must, as in:	
You must report to—	Are required to report to—
You must have—	Are required to have—or— Shall have as a part of—
This is a must—	Is part of required procedure—or— you can consider this as a minimum
Sorry, as in:	
Response to an error—	I, we regret (this oversight) or (inconvenience)
Apology for behavior—	I, regret my unwise choice
Responding to behavior— of other—i.e. I'm sorry you feel that way	I, regret anything (action) we might have done to cause you to feel that way

Conventional Phrase	Options
So What's Your Point?—	Could you run that by me one more time— or—I'm not sure I see the whole picture—or—Could you describe that one more time
I Don't Understand You—	For purpose of clarity could we go over this one more time

Conventional Phrase	Options
I'm Sorry It Took So Long—	I (we) appreciate your patience—and
These Are Our Policies—	Here are the options which I (we) can offer at this time
Could you:	
Slow down or lower your voice—	I appreciate your bringing this to my (our) attention—and now I need your help (pause)
Watch your language—	I was unable to get all of your helpful information (ask to repeat)—or—I perceive this has you quite upset
Wrong, as in:	
You did it wrong—	Not quite correct
That was a wrong thing to do—	Inappropriate thing
It's all wrong—	A more appropriate action might be
Right, as in:	
You were right—	Your actions seem appropriate
That's the right thing to do—	It appears that the wisest (most appropriate) thing (action)
Which is—Right—	Which is the most appropriate, (wisest) choice

Love Language and the Affirmation Process

The use of love language supports the affirmation process. **Did your eyes flutter when you saw the word "love"?** If so, you are value judging the term before you understand how I am using it.

Love has been described as being on three levels. The first level, filial love, is what we extend to our families, or it can be developed within a business, church, or neighborhood environment. The most important aspect of filial love is accepting another person, not condemning or disqualifying them. The second level is *eros* (romantic love). The third level is *agape*, the ability to extend yourself without expecting or anticipating anything. This is the most difficult level of love to achieve. Working to get to that level may be a lifetime challenge.

People tend to be uncomfortable with the term "love language" because they associate it with romantic love. As I use it here, "love" is the ability to extend yourself to nurture another human being or yourself. If that is still difficult for you, when I say "love," think "care."

When a service rep responds to angry callers with "I can tell that you are upset," "I regret this occurred, and I truly appreciate that you have called it to our attention," or "I regret that our actions, however unintentional, created this discomfort," he/she is using a form of love language (which is also persuasive and affirming).

You can apply love language to employees who underperform, are tardy, or have created a problem. If you intend to maintain the relationship with the employee, separate the behavior from the person and affirm the individual while denying the behavior.

At his lectures, the great behaviorist Dr. William Glasser used to say, "The more a person perceives that he/she is loved the less they will interfere with the lives of others."

Case #202: The New Language of Management

While conducting a management seminar aimed at improving language, I utilized the following tactic.

At 4:30 p.m. I ended the session and gave the forty-five attending managers, all of whom were male, an assignment that was met with groans and snickers.

I asked them to call home and recite the following to their spouse or significant other: "I've been thinking about our relationship and I wanted to tell you the three reasons that I believe our being together is one of the greatest decisions I ever made."

Next they were asked to enumerate three reasons—examples such as:

- "Your thoughtfulness"
- "The way you problem solve"
- "The way you respond to my needs and feelings"

They were asked to think about actual examples to go with these statements. The final step was to end by saying, "It is important for me to tell you this and to let you know how much I love you." I told them we would resume discussion about these issues after our group dinner at about 7 p.m.

When I resumed after dinner, I asked, "How many of you completed your assignment and made the call as directed?" About 60 percent of their hands were raised.

When I asked why those not raising their hands did not follow through, the responses included statements such as:

- "I had other business calls and ran out of time."
- "I had other priorities."
- "I got sidetracked."

A few admitted their discomfort with the assignment or did not consider it valuable to their participation in the seminar.

Next, I asked the twenty-six or so who had followed through, "How many of you followed the script pretty much as suggested?" This time about ten hands were raised. The sixteen who didn't follow through had their reasons, such as:

- "I was uncomfortable with much of the language."
- "My wife (or significant other) knows how I feel, so I changed some of the language."

The crowning moment came when one of the cooperative managers recited how he had followed directions and described the outcome. He said: "When I finished, which was by no means easy, I waited for a positive response. However, my wife said, 'The day started badly with a flat tire, our daughter had a fever, and in my hurry to get to the pharmacy, I was stopped and given a speeding ticket. Then I had an argument on the phone with my sister. Now, on top of everything, you call and you're drunk.'"

Naturally this got a big laugh. Yet, even this humor helped me make my case.

First, I acknowledged the difficulty in using a language style that is new, different, or at least inconsistent with one's usual style. Then, I reminded these forty-five managers that they were attending a program intended to help them understand improved communication and to develop familiarity with love (care) language. The exercise they had just completed, or failed to complete, was designed to help them understand the complexity of learning how to use this language for managing and training.

Now, if they found it difficult to use love (care) language with someone they knew intimately, with whom they had deep personal experiences, positive and negative, imagine how difficult it might be to use what they would learn on employees, associates, customers, and suppliers.

The truth is that learning sensitivity, compassion, and care language is difficult, and more so for men than women.

Case #314: Love Language Takes Guts

Once, during a presentation to a large international company, I referred several times to love language. I described it and suggested it sometimes even meant being tactile—touching another person. Following the speech, when the applause died down, the CEO of the company came to the lectern to close that portion of the conference.

He said, "I'd like to thank Mr. Yoho. I do appreciate the enthusiasm and humor that he brought to our meeting." Then he looked into the center of the audience, and with a little laugh he said, "But I will tell you in advance, if any one of you ever comes up to me and says, 'I love you,' I will punch you in the mouth."

That same evening I had dinner with the CEO and his board of directors. At the table he said to me, "Mr. Yoho, what kind of corporations have you run?" I described my various job roles. Then he said, "I am curious about your language here today. How did you run your companies?"

I said, "Pretty much the way you run yours today. For the most part people were afraid to talk back to me or question my decisions. I set the tone and the rules, and mostly it got me positive results and nobody would dare challenge me. So their only alternative was to dig in and make it work. However, I never got the complete truth or openness from my managers. We were successful. Yet, I believe, we could have done better, quicker, if I had learned about love (care) language earlier in my career." He smiled and shook my hand, although I am not sure he got my message. He was not about to change. He conveyed the sense that love, sensitivity, and nurturing were anathema to his feelings, and that he would feel demeaned by their presence in his management style.

Answering Questions with Questions. Good love or care language often involves answering questions with questions (see chapter 7 on selling). Most people are not taught to sell. Many think that because they know how to speak, they know how to sell.

> Salespeople have to be taught to use effective language because they are constantly meeting new people, yet using the same language they utilize in social conversation. Frequently they don't get the outcomes they desire.

When you are positive, you understand what the other party said, yet you respond by saying, "Run that by me one more time." That is an effective use of love language. You are saying, "I am interested, I want to listen, tell me again." If done effectively, no one gets upset about repeating or extending what they have told you.

Can you completely understand others based on their one-time explanation of what they want or will do? It's doubtful. Remember that the most commonly used words in the English language often have multiple meanings. In fact, the 500 most commonly used words collectively have 16,000 different definitions.

Even if you are highly educated and use 3 to 4 percent of the 550,000 or more words in the average dictionary, you are still only using 15,000 to 20,000 words, which means **there are over 500,000 words that you don't know or don't use**. You can't assume that you fully understand most phrases, whether it sounds or appears simple or not.

> The use of love or care language helps to ensure that you understand the other party. No matter how clear or distinct another person is when they tell you something, it behooves you to ask additional questions to clarify your understanding.

Listening and Questioning Usually Lead to Processing. How do you know if a person is really listening to you when you are talking? Ask an open-ended question (one that can't be answered with a simple yes or no) and wait for a response. You can determine quickly if he is thinking about something totally different while putting up an effective front that conveys he is listening.

People who nod, or essentially repeat what you say, aren't necessarily listening. You say the bus is late and someone says, "Yes, the bus is always late." This is low-level communication; it may be socially acceptable, yet little meaningful exchange of ideas is taking place.

To become a good communicator, listen first, then ask questions. You will increase your understanding of the other person's message before you reply.

If I say to you, "The traffic was bad this morning," a question that indicates that you are listening and want to understand further would be, "What did you notice about the traffic this morning that was worse than usual?"

Effective language is measured very simply. Can the person to whom you are speaking truly understand what you are saying? If he or she can, then you can take that person from one level to the next. Most effective communicators modify their language to the level of the listener. They speak on the level at which they know the listener can respond. Here is an example via a joke on the need for correct language:

> At a time of grave crisis during the Civil War, President Lincoln was contacted by an opportunist who reported that the head of customs had just died. He asked, "Mr. President, would it be all right if I took his place?" "Well," said Lincoln, "if it's all right with the undertaker, it's all right with me."

Case #414: Selected Appearances and Selected Material

There are many options regarding the type of language that one uses and how it's used. Former President Ronald Reagan made it a practice to personally deliver good news to the nation. When bad news had to be dispensed, he would rely on someone from the State Department to deliver it at a press conference. We quickly became conditioned so that any time Reagan spoke, we knew that the message would be positive and uplifting. Perhaps they called him the great communicator not so much for what he said as for what he didn't say.

The use of effective and appropriate language has a double payoff. It creates more positive outcomes, and the by-product of this will be a greater feeling of accomplishment and feeling of well-being.

EPOD Tactics

- To increase your vocabulary, select two or three words weekly. Print them on three-by-five cards along with their definition and force them into your language.

- The language we learn as children is usually the same language we will use as managers, until we learn more effective communication skills.
- When you require more information, ask an open-ended question.
- Avoid using the words "should," "ought," and "must" in your directives.
- Emulate Socrates. He asked more, listened more, taught more, yet said less.
- If you want to understand your employees or your associates, let them talk about their childhood and their time growing up. What you are looking at is a grown-up version of what they were.
- Retain some of your childlike qualities. They can be helpful when you want to encourage creativity and spontaneity.
- Practice using love (care) language. Extend yourself to one another, then listen to how people respond. Practice being appreciative of what people tell you, even if it is not what you want to hear.
- Work on improving your interpersonal communications. Use a different vocabulary. Use a nurturing tone.
- The best way to get others to use new behavior is to first adopt the behavior yourself. Then you become a model for others.
- Can you forgive without conditions or justification? If you say to someone, "I forgive you, but," the word "but" serves as an eraser by wiping out all that came before it. True forgiveness occurs without "but."
- Don't refer to employees/associates as "subordinates." Think for a moment about getting high-level performance from someone labeled and functioning as a sub (below par) ordinate.
- Remember, the essence of all communication is the outcome you receive. If you are not getting the outcome you desire, change your communication.

CHAPTER 12

The Human Difference

"A true test of strong management is, how will you convince others to do that which is in their own best interest?"
—*Dave Yoho*, Managing Yourself & Others

Have you ever noticed that when a new coach takes over a team, and the team starts winning, people are inclined to say it must be the coach? I maintain that it is not the coach but the players—more precisely the way the players respond to the dynamics of the new situation and the changes in the culture.

Case #432: Interim Coach Wins It All

Before the start of the 1989 NCAA Basketball Tournament, Michigan Wolverine coach Bill Frieder announced that he had accepted the head coaching position at Arizona State for the next season, whereupon he was immediately replaced with an interim coach. The Wolverines went on to win the NCAA title. The interim coach, Steve Fisher, who was then made full-time coach, was credited with doing an excellent job and rightfully so. Was it purely brilliant coaching that made the difference, or were there other factors at work? If the situation received extensive and often negative media coverage, and the fans expressed deep concern that the team was handicapped by issues including the sudden coaching change, these are mitigating factors.

Then, as an aftermath, basics were reintroduced by management and numerous minor adjustments were made within the culture. The combination of all these factors, including the new persona of management (the coach), encouraged members of the team to buckle down, enhance their skills, and try harder.

Many football franchises have witnessed the arrival of a new coach who leads the team to a winning season following a losing season. Most people say it's purely the new coach; prevailing wisdom says it is the players, how they respond to the new coach, and how they regard themselves and the coach.

Frequently, in the second year, the coach does not equal the success of the previous season despite the fact that most of the same elements, including the players, are the same.

The Human Difference in Business

In business, when the same plant and the same employees operate under new management, they frequently begin to respond and react differently and have a record quarter or year. This type of phenomena tells us that people—the team or the staff, as well as the coach or the management—do indeed make the difference.

I frequently compare retail shopping experiences. Granted, I may not be totally objective. I like Nordstrom's—the design and style of their stores and the quality of their merchandise. I believe Nordstrom's employees respond and react to customers in an exceptional manner, making employees in other stores seem ordinary. However, most large retail companies hire the same type of salespeople, with similar backgrounds, education and experience. I believe the difference is in the way that they have been trained and managed to handle their jobs.

The difference between retail environments is very dramatic in terms of the amount of sales that are generated. Most upscale stores are very well lit and carry excellent products, yet as discussed previously, many people consistently find themselves feeling more upbeat while shopping in Nordstrom's.

An individual can make a dramatic impact on those around her by drawing upon the elements of EPOD, even if she is less skilled or experienced than others.

Case #331: No One Told Him to Do It

In a letter to the editor of a mid-sized city newspaper, a writer commended a specific bus driver who worked for the public transit system. The writer commented how the public transit's buses were overcrowded, dirty, and ran late. However, he cited one driver by name, who had a pleasant word for everyone as they stepped on board his bus.

He explained, if this bus driver runs into a traffic jam he reassures his passengers by saying, "Well, we have another little problem here, but don't worry. We are going to make it pretty much on time." The writer went on to say, "I find myself waiting for *his* bus to come along while letting others pass by."

Who makes the service difference? The transit system? The bus? I believe the combination of the driver and the people on the bus are the answer. The people on the bus respond to the environment created by this driver, and they affirm him. The process then becomes reciprocal.

Human Resource Development Is Behind Much Corporate Success

Why do the human resource development (HRD) skills of Walt Disney, Lee Iacocca, or Richard DeVos, former chairman of Amway, get interpreted as something else? Disney's success is attached primarily to his creative genius; Iacocca's to his marketing know-how; DeVos's to his unique sales methodology and motivational techniques.

These visible talents are minor compared to the phenomenal success of each of the men in developing and using human resources.

In my observation of the Japanese management techniques which were lauded in the 1980s and '90s, 90 percent of the success of their methods was related to HRD. Yet the understanding of HRD was around for years in the United States. Why was it so difficult to sell it to business and industry?

Many companies lack the skill and know-how to implement HRD programs, and thousands of small businesses still cannot identify the process within their own companies.

Some aspects of HRD are so simple they are ignored; many businesses prefer to focus on complex management concepts. The more complex the process, the more accomplished management appears to be, whether they are or not.

A growing number of key management executives thwart their company's ability to recognize that the key to their success is through an uncomplicated HRD process that a high school graduate can understand and put into practice.

Most people can be in the presence of great ideas and never recognize them because of resistance to or fear of change.

Training Is Crucial. The key to staffing in most companies is finding people who are trainable. A successful business manager or entrepreneur recognizes that in today's fast-paced society, more than ever, it is necessary to train your staff for the job you offer. Irrespective of the skill level that they bring to your company, trainable people can make the difference that adds up to success.

If you are hiring bank tellers, look beyond the ability to run a computer-driven teller's machine, examine checks, and properly handle cash. (Yes, these skills are important.) Examine those applicants high in people skills, who can make customers feel good about being in the bank. New tellers have to be trained to use effective language, to be effective for a modern financial institution.

Those who hire people to serve as toll collectors need to find people with relatively low energy and high patience, who do not get bored easily. Those who will turn on the radio or read a few pages of a magazine when it gets slow, but who do not need to leave the booth regularly to converse with coworkers. In any position, there is a definite behavioral style that fits the individual best suited for the job.

Effective Hiring: Will You Know It When You See It?

How do you avoid hiring the wrong people?

In seminars, I frequently project an image that shows a well-dressed man sitting across the table from a job applicant who looks very similar. The caption in the photo says, "I like your looks."

Andrew Carnegie, founder of U.S. Steel, confessed that he knew little about the steel business. His great strength was selecting people who had the ability to do the required job. Carnegie was a rare exception. Most large companies have human resource departments whose job it is to fill positions by finding the right person with the appropriate skill and behavior.

In evaluating human resource potential, including your own, it is risky to proceed using intuition or gut feeling. Many top CEOs tell me that they have uncanny powers when it comes to picking the right people. Yet high turnover at all levels of management plagues many industries, and at lower levels employee turnover is an insidious problem.

Curb Your Intuition. Many employers in small companies use their intuition combined with interviews, resumes, applications, references, and other marginally useful indicators. They might say, "I talked to him for forty-five minutes and he has a good background. I read his resume. I think he can do well here; he seems to be the kind of person we are looking for."

Intuition serves us well in some instances; however, when hiring, intuition alone begets many mis-hires.

The Human Difference in Growing from Small to Large

For a small company to grow into a large company it takes people. One of the primary methods of bringing people on board is to devise a job description that precisely defines what the task and skill capabilities are that will enable them to successfully execute the responsibilities of that particular job.

This is obviously not earth-shattering news. However, most job descriptions are based on the employer's perception of the job role. To determine if a job description is working, ask your current employees to write their description of the job position they are now fulfilling and see if it matches your description.

Particularly in smaller companies, job descriptions are not used. However, even a simple, one-page series of bullets defining the job role and expectations is better than nothing at all. Still, too often people are hired based on notions of what is wanted, needed, or expected. Employers and employees alike can benefit from what I call a script for performance.

In analyzing the type of performance you seek for an existing job, start with the people you already employ. Develop a grading chart that rates each staff person in areas in which they are expected to perform, by several criteria. Use a grading system of 1 (low) to 10 (high). As with any grading system, bias can occur. Nevertheless, the goal is to record how you view an employee's performance in each specific aspect of the job function.

If someone is graded low in customer relations, work with that person in that one area to improve specific performance.

A Self-Prepared Script for Your Performance. You can develop your own script of performance. First, you can devise your own grading chart, which is particularly useful if your employer doesn't use one. As objectively as possible, grade yourself in the multitude of areas that are required for you to successfully complete your job; self-assessment requires personal discipline.

> Most people don't want to take the time to assess themselves and they certainly don't want to give themselves a low score.

If asked about your skill in customer relations, chances are you have a decent idea as to whether you are good, fair, or poor. If you are fair or below, spend the next twenty-one days focusing your attention on improving your ability to handle customers. Put a note on your desk that says, "The customer is the key," or something of a similar nature. Don't try to handle too many areas of improvement at once; usually one will be more than enough.

The grading chart serves its purpose, but the objectivity of an outside evaluation can't be understated.

The Importance of Defining the Job and Accompanying Behaviors. Your behavioral style is something that you develop which enables you to deal with your environment. Behavior is not good or bad, it just is. If you are the eighth child in your family, your behavior will be different from that of your siblings because your parents were different people at different stages of their lives, and your addition to the family altered its structure.

As an employer, if you can simply define the responsibilities of a job and then identify the behavioral profile of the person who could function well in that job role, you would have greater potential to achieve an excellent job-to-person match.

> When we work with a client who is attempting to bring on board the right staff, the first thing we do is determine the ideal profile of the person they are seeking.

We ask the client, "What exactly do you want this person to be able to do?" "What kind of temperament should he have?"

and "Who will she report to?" We ask them to make the list as long and as specific as possible.

When making their list, we suggest observing employees who are already successful in the job function. Often they can identify the degree of creativity needed and the organizational capability, responsiveness, stamina, interpersonal skills, and ability of the individual who is right for the job. Then we use an evaluation tool to assess various individuals. The evaluation tells us three basic things:

- How they perceive themselves (a clue to how they will normally function).
- How they will operate under undue stress.
- How they will mask behavior to meet the needs of group.

Ascertaining Behavioral Style

Many private services provide behavioral indexes that help to ascertain behavioral style: how one interacts with other people, how one tends to function in general, and how one tends to function under stress. I recommend the use of a behavioral profile that is self-administered.

I rely upon a preestablished evaluation tool when hiring new employees/associates because we are all creatures of habit with deep-seated prejudices, many of which we are not even aware. Often, we hire those who mirror our manner of dress, speech, or expression, when their skills, attitudes, and experience may not match the type of position we are seeking to fill. I use behavioral profiles both within my own company and in working with clients. I advise chief executive officers and top managers to take the profile first so that they can better understand their preferences and working styles and how those match up with other people. This activity enables them to better identify the type of individual who is likely to have the right background and disposition for a specific job, as well as the type of individual who tends to work more harmoniously in conjunction with the boss's style.

Whether or not you run your own business or department, or even manage others, I suggest that you treat yourself to some type of job-related evaluation tool. It is in your long-term best interest to understand how you will tend to interact with others in the workplace and what types of tasks suit you. The evaluation tool yields objective information regarding your strengths and weaknesses, likes and dislikes, and often reveals information not otherwise easily surfaced.

Not Hiring in the Dark. In smaller organizations, hiring someone is analogous to developing a close personal relationship. When you hire someone you have to tolerate their behavior, and they have to tolerate yours. Ergo, to be an effective manager requires understanding yourself, the kind of person you are, and the kind of people you can tolerate.

Before you can become an effective manager, you have to know what you are managing. What are your employees' likes and dislikes? How are they likely to respond under pressure? The time to find out these things is not six or nine months down the pike, but when a new person first comes on board.

Everybody Fits Someplace. The beauty of profiling instruments is that they offer the potential to place each person in that environment where they are best suited.

I encounter people who get their degree, enter a profession (even law or medicine), and later realize that it is not what they want to be doing. Yet they are locked into a career at age thirty or thirty-five and spend years doing what they don't want to do.

Case #23: Help Talent to Excel through Proper Placement

Vince Lombardi, the fabled NFL coach, had a great football player named Paul Hornung while at Green Bay. Hornung was the Heisman Trophy winner at Notre Dame and was one of the most talented players to ever play the game. When he came out of Notre Dame he was a quarterback, but he was capable of playing fullback, halfback, tight end, and kicker. Lombardi assessed Hornung's capabilities and concluded that he would become a halfback who could kick field goals. As a halfback Hornung went on to become a Hall of Famer. Regardless of the skill level of your employees, when you find the right position for them you enhance the possibility of their moving from mediocrity to greatness.

Once you determine someone's behavioral style and place them into a position that matches it, they will bloom like a flower.

Case #148: People Did Make the Difference

Albert Madway operated a chain of dry cleaning stores situated on busy thoroughfares in strip malls, offering one-day service for dry cleaning and shirt laundering. A key ingredient to Madway's operation was each store's manager, who oversaw two or three full-time employees and up to seven part-timers.

Each store was connected by a computer to his plant, and he received daily readouts on each store's activity, which provided a simple means of tracking individual customers' orders (useful if there is a glitch) and of maintaining cash control.

Shortly after the computer was installed, Madway noticed that the newest and most remote store in the chain was experiencing the most sizeable business increase for four months in a row.

The store had an interim manager, a woman named Edie. The original manager had quit, and Edie, who had been working at the store since it opened, was thrown into the job although she did not come from a business or managerial background.

She was a bright, sharp woman who had returned to outside work after her three children had matured. Knowing little about the intricacies of the dry cleaning business, except for what she had been shown, she concentrated her time and effort in the front of the store with customers.

Edie attempted to greet each customer, ask their names, and inquire about other interests. She passed out candy to their children, offered comments on the clothing brought in, and encouraged the other employees to do likewise. Whenever minor problems occurred, she called the customers, assured them of a swift resolution, and expressed appreciation for their patronage.

Edie's progression to manager was a quirk; no one else was available at the time to fulfill the function. Later when she was profiled, all the indicators pointed to her being a "people person" rather than a "process person," a key attribute in a business where personal contact is of paramount importance.

Like Edie, those who function with self-appreciation (self-love) have the appropriate behavior to stimulate the same kind of feelings in customers and prospects. However, many prospective employees do not emanate from an environment of love and are therefore incapable of fulfilling this function without training.

An observation of Dr. Bernie Siegel, author of a 1990s' bestseller entitled *Love, Medicine, and Miracles* (Harper & Row, 1986) helps to further explain why the Edies of the world tend to be the exceptions:

"The hardest lesson for me to learn was that most of my patients are not the products of such love," says Dr. Siegel. "In fact I would estimate that 80 percent of my patients saw themselves as unwanted or treated indifferently as children."

Because not all people are capable of using behavior that will stimulate positive interaction, the challenge is to find those who are open to new ideas and language restructuring.

In almost every case where we are retained to work on turnarounds, we don't start dealing with products, advertising, or sales presentations. We find that by stimulating the properly selected person to effectively follow our new business plan, we achieve early and profitable results.

EPOD Tactics

- I am appalled by the number of people who don't answer mail or return phone calls; my most successful clients answer every letter and respond to every phone call personally or by delegation, no matter how insignificant it appears.
- Behind every letter and phone call is a person. Let them know you appreciate their interest.

- If you want to greatly influence people, stop trying to change them. Change the way you interact with them.
- The key ingredients in evaluating people for the job role are:
  - Can they do the job?
  - Will they do the job?
  - Do they fit?
- Reevaluate a resume after you have completed the first phone interview with the candidate.
- Consider the hidden factors that people can bring to a job role.
- In many cases a simple "test" in the job role will determine the capabilities and learning capacities of the applicant.
- Observe these immutable laws for hiring:
  1. Self-starters seldom do.
  2. After numerous interviews or few applicants, less qualified candidates look better.
  3. The ideal candidate usually isn't.
  4. The majority of resumes received seldom match the job description in your ad. The best resumes are frequently a product of creative writing and vivid imaginations.
  5. The best candidates for your job are probably already working for someone else.
  6. "What ever happened to what's-his-name?" is the sequel to last year's great hiring story.
  7. Hiring the right salesperson takes twice the time you expected and much more time than you have.
  8. Poor performers seem to surface soon after a sixty-day probation period ends.
  9. The true cost of mis-hires doesn't show up on your P&L.
  10. Your gut feelings work best when they indicate it's time for lunch, and seldom when it comes to choosing the best candidate.

11. Unless the interviewer has been trained in the recruiting process, mis-hires become the rule rather than the exception.
12. A candidate's true behavior is usually masked during an interview and can be discovered either by a profile or by disappointment after training has been completed.

- Hold regular input meetings. Ask employees in small groups to provide suggestions for improving the work environment, upgrading efficiency, and reducing costs. Reward each idea submitted with $2, each idea used with $10–$25, and the best idea after six months with $100.
- Have an affirmation meeting, where one employer is singled out and bombarded with anaffirmation which starts with, "I appreciate you (John/Mary) because . . ."

CONCLUSION

Don't Let Your Dream Die

> "Faith is believing in things when common sense tells you not to."
>
> —*Anonymous*

There are so many untold stories of greatness. Some are coupled with false starts that would tend to make success seem a distant, unreachable goal.

It is often difficult to remember that all great movements started with a simple idea. Between the idea and its fulfillment were hurdles, barriers, setbacks, and disappointments.

The examples and case histories within this book are meant to continually serve as reminders. They can become encouragement when all that seems to be around you is negativity and gloom.

I leave you with two simple examples of positivity that grew out of pain.

As a youngster I read *Don Quixote*. Later, as an adult, I saw the musical adaptation, *The Man of LaMancha,* and I was moved by the enchanting words of the song, "The Impossible Dream." The words are so beautiful, could they be about a crazed nobleman? It is believed that the words to "The Impossible Dream" were written about Miguel Cervantes, the author of *Don Quixote*. As a young man, Cervantes was taken prisoner in the Spanish-Moorish Wars. Eventually he was ransomed with fees paid by his family. Upon his return home, he was appointed as a tax collector.

When he attempted to collect from the rich and the church instead of the poor, he was imprisoned and tortured, this time in his own country. His choice was to remain optimistic and disciplined instead of becoming hateful, despondent, or worse.

Cervantes wrote *Don Quixote* as a social protest, and it has lasted hundreds of years. His writings were directed toward a positive, energetic persuasion, teeming with optimism and mirroring his disciplines.

Life is complicated and can leave you feeling like you are out of the loop. You may feel the need to condemn your past, how others have treated you, or the social injustice that often prevails.

Life is not fair. Everyone may not receive the same opportunities or treatment. Some live through their setbacks and disappointments, some become bitter or shallow, and some like Cervantes turn their social protest into success.

What will be your social protest? Will you live amidst the pain of whatever it is you are experiencing, or will you take the opportunity to write your own song and fulfill your dream?

When Rudyard Kipling was a boy, he lived in India with his father, a British Army colonel, and he saw the English soldier, guardian of the British Empire, as highly important. He came to love and revere the English soldier, and later in life wrote affectionately of the soldier's life.

Among the many disappointments in his life was seeing soldiers treated with disrespect when they returned to their sovereign soil. He also saw his own words, misused, altered, plagiarized, rebuked, reviled, and even censured. At the moment of his greatest pain, while suffering the loss of a young daughter, he wrote the words to the very moving poem, "If":

> If you can keep your head when all about you
> Are losing theirs and blaming it on you,
> If you can trust yourself when all men doubt you
> But make allowance for their doubting too,
> If you can wait and not be tired by waiting,
> Or being lied about, don't deal in lies,

Or being hated, don't give way to hating,
And yet don't look too good, nor talk too wise:

If you can dream—and not make dreams your master,
If you can think—and not make thoughts your aim;
If you can meet with Triumph and Disaster
And treat those two impostors just the same;
If you can bear to hear the truth you've spoken
Twisted by knaves to make a trap for fools,
Or watch the things you gave your life to, broken,
And stoop and build 'em up with worn-out tools:

If you can make one heap of all your winnings
And risk it all on one turn of pitch-and-toss,
And lose, and start again at your beginnings
And never breath a word about your loss;
If you can force your heart and nerve and sinew
To serve your turn long after they are gone,
And so hold on when there is nothing in you
Except the Will which says to them: "Hold on!"

If you can talk with crowds and keep your virtue,
Or walk with kings—nor lose the common touch,
If neither foes nor loving friends can hurt you;
If all men count with you, but none too much,
If you can fill the unforgiving minute
With sixty seconds' worth of distance run,
Yours is the Earth and everything that's in it,
And—which is more—you'll be a Man, my son!

—Rudyard Kipling

Those words are virtually a treatise on the EPOD Theory. They emphasize positivity. The very recitation of the words will raise your level of energy. Throughout the poem there is the thread of optimism and the belief in a brighter tomorrow. Whenever I recite this to audiences with background music, I alter the reference to "man" and add the words "and woman" because I know that the words apply to my brothers and sisters alike.

And—what of you? When your day or your life is not what you want it to be, will you remember that God made you so different, so beautifully different, that even your fingerprints are unique? May the concept of EPOD cause you to remember:

You are unique and special, and you have the potential to be whatever it is you want to be.

Dave Yoho is what he writes about. He believes achievement is a journey—not a destination. He credits his experiences growing up on the streets of inner city Philadelphia as getting a Ph.D. in street smarts. He attended Temple University night school while holding down a full time job, and throughout his formal education he believed every step no matter how difficult paid off handsomely. He is proud to relate how his penchant for reading and research coupled with his ability to retain information has enabled him to combine formal education with street savvy to jump start a highly successful business career.

Dave's first job after graduation was a trainee salesman in a company which soon became a division of Reynolds Aluminum. He rapidly became one of the top ten salesmen in its 500-man sales organization and went on to become a branch manager within two years. By age 25 he was part of its executive management team. At 27 he left to start his own business which, by the time he sold his interests in it 22 years later, had become a $60 million volume conglomerate.

Now President and CEO of a consulting company which represents Fortune 500 companies as well as many moderate and small size businesses, Dave has delivered 5,000 speeches at conventions and seminars in all 50 states and in 18 countries. He has appeared in over 100 training video series for corporations and his first book, How to Have a Good Year Every Year (Berkley Press, 1991), became a best seller.

Dave Yoho Associates—Fairfax, VA
Phone: (703) 591-2490
Fax: (703) 273-6626
Website: daveyoho.com
Email: dave@daveyoho.com

INDEX

ACID (Arouse, Cultivate, Information, Determine) Test, the, 141–43
  within a nurturing environment, 142–43
Albertson, Joe, 104
Amway Corporation, 103
Audi, 132–34

Behavioral kinesiology (BK), 18, 19
  implementing a personal regime of, 26–27
Behavioral Kinesiology (Diamond), 20
Bogues, Tyrone (Muggsy), 102
Bremner, John, 191
Buchwald, Art, 174
Buffet, Warren, 148
Butler, Samuel, 147

Canfield, Jack, 184–85
Carnegie, Andrew, 231
Century 21 Real Estate, 109
C.E.O. Logic (Johnson), 70
Cervantes, Miguel, 241–42
Chicken Soup for the Soul (Canfield and Hansen), 184–85
Chrysler Corporation, 53–55, 53–55, 169–71
Churchill, Winston, 190
Cialdini, Robert, 32–33, 189–90
Circuit City Stores, 105
Clinton, Bill, 152
Coachmen Industries, 69
Colter, Larraine, 115

Communication. *See* Effective Communication
Cyclops Steel, 108

Dayton-Hudson Corporation, 104
Depression, 59–60
DeVos, Richard, 229
Diamond, John, 20, 25
Discipline, 69. *See also* rule changing, and discipline
  as a crucial business element, 72–74
  and delegation to others, 77–78, 80–82
  disciplining yourself, 82–83
  fundamental disciplines, 74–75
  internal or external, 82
  to lose weight, 83–84
  and planning, 97
  and public speaking, 202–3
Disney, Walt, 229
Domino's Pizza, 104
Don Quixote (Cervantes), 241–42
Drucker, Peter, 148–49, 151
Dyer, Wayne, 59

Effective communication, 207, 209–11, 214–15
  and affirming language, 211–14
  answering questions with questions, 222–23
  listening and processing, 223
  and love language, 218–22
  and the use of clichés, 207, 208–9
  and value judging, 215–16

INDEX

Einstein, Albert, 207
Energy, 9–10, 151. *See also* Left- and right-brain thinking
  and the ability to choose, 19
  and being centered,
  and customer greetings, 13
  determining personal level of, 27–28
  as elective, 16–17
  and emotional states, 25
  and the high-energy approach, 12–13
  and the illusion of a high-energy environment, 10–12
  maintaining, 17–19
  and nutrition, 20–21
  personal, 20
  and public speaking, 190–92
  transmitting, 15–16
EPOD Theory (Energy, Persuasion, Optimism, Discipline), xi, 1–2, 169, 241–44. *See also* Discipline; Energy; Optimism; Persuasion; Selling, and EPOD solutions
  application of in business, 147–51
    and contracts, 151–53
    and exploitation, 153–55
    and value systems, 155–60
    and working with accountants, 160–61, 162
    and working with consultants, 160–61, 163–65
    and working with lawyers, 160–62
  becoming and EPOD person, 4–5
  being aware of what you speak and think, 5
  being your best, 5–6
  deciding about today, 6–7
  introduction to main elements of, 3–4
  tactics, 29–30, 46–47, 66–67, 86, 99, 118–19, 143–45, 165–67, 187–88, 203–5, 224–25, 237–39
  understanding and utilizing, 2–3
Erroneous Zones (Dyer), 59–60
Everett, Edward, 194, 195

Federal Express Corporation, 104
Fiore, Jack, 126
Fisher, Steve, 227
Ford Motor Company, 180–81
Fosbury, Dick, 110
Frankl, Viktor, 19
Franks, Paul, 70–72
Frieder, Bill, 227

Gandhi. *See* Mahatma Gandhi
Garden State Brickface, 76
Gates, Bill, 148
GEICO Insurance, 104
Gettysburg Address, the, 194–97
Glasser, William, 218
Goodwin, Leo, 104
Gove, Bill, 198
Gross, Murray, 106–9

Hansen, Mark Victor, 184–85
Harris, Louis, 60–61
Have a Great Year Every Year (Yoho), ix–xi
Hayes, Ira, 176
Heaney, Peter, 78–80
Hitler, Adolf, 192–93
Home Depot, 109
Horatio Alger Award, 174, 185
Hornung, Paul, 235–36
How to Have a Good Year Every Year (Yoho), 214
Hudson, Joseph, 104
Human difference, the, 227–28
  and ascertaining behavioral style, 234–35
  in business, 228–29
  and effective hiring, 231
  and curbing intuition, 231–32

growing from small to large, 232
  and job definition, 233–34
  and a self-prepared script, 232–33
  and human resource development (HRD), 229–30
  and staffing, 230

Iacocca, Lee, 53–55, 169–71, 229
Influence—The Science and Practice (Cialdini), 32, 189–90
Inside America (Harris), 60

Jacoby, Aaron, 96
Jarvis, Charles W., 198–99
Johnson, C. Ray, 69–70
Jolson, Marvin, 128
Jones, Curt, 36–39

Ketner, Brown, 104
Ketner, Ralph, 104
Kiernan, Greg, 76
King, Martin Luther, Jr., 171, 190
Kipling, Rudyard, 1, 72, 242–43

Learned Optimism (Seligman), 50
Left- and right-brain thinking, 23–24
  achieving hemispheric balance, 24–25
  characteristics of, 24
Lincoln, Abraham, 60, 193, 194–95, 223
Lombardi, Vince, 235–36
Love, Medicine, and Miracles (Siegel), 25, 237

Madway, Albert, 236–37
Mahatma Gandhi, 171
Marriot, J. Willard, 149–50
Martin, Alice, 43–44
McGrane, William, 113–14
Melani Brothers, 58
Miller, Alice, 212

Mitchell, W., 181–83
Monaghan, Thomas, 104
Moore, David, 75–77
Mother Teresa, 171
Movers and shakers, 169–71
  common denominators of, 174–77
  doing things uniquely, 171–74
  and innovation, 176
  recognizing, 177–78
  and risk, 180–85
  in the speaking profession, 178–80
  and women in management, 185–87
Murphy, Bob, 63

Neall, George M., 126–28
Nordstrom's department stores, 14, 228

O'Brien, Bob, 105–6
Olson, Bob, 110–12
Optimism, 49–51, 151. *See also* rule changing, and optimism
  approaching each day with, 60–61
  creating long-term customers with, 62–63
  and your feelings about yourself, 55–56
  and fighting depression, 59–60
  and public speaking, 197–202
  starting each day with, 61–62
  and taking action, 60
Orben, Robert, 199–201

Peale, Norman Vincent, x–xi, 171–72, 190
Peck, M. Scott, 57, 172
Penny, J. C., 175
Perdue, Frank, 175
Persuasion, 31. *See also* Jones, Curt; Power Linguistics™
  and customer needs, 41–42

Persuasion (*continued*)
   and effective customer service departments, 43–45
   and hedging language, 35
   non-persuasive language, 35–36
   and potential, 39–41
   and preparation, 39
   and public speaking, 192–97
   removing blocks to persuasive language, 33–35
Pessimism, 50, 60
Power Linguistics™, 31–32, 130, 190, 209, 213, 216
   and de-persuasive language, 33–34
   resistance to, 140–41
   and sales training, 131, 136–40
Power plans, 87–88
   and discipline, 97
   financial power planning, 92
     establish credit, 92–93
     and IRAs, 93
     and savings bonds, 93
   need for, 88–89
   planning for growth, 90–92
   planning as helpful, 89
   planning for when money arrives, 93–94
   and the rule of 72, 94–97
   simple systems of, 89–90
Power Statements, 122
   #1, 124–28
   #2, 128–32
   #3, 132
   #4, 132, 136
   #5, 136
Prisoners of Childhood (Miller), 212

Rales, Norman, 172–74
Rapport, 129
Reagan, Ronald, 224
Real estate purchases, 160
Representational information, 144, 144n

Road Less Traveled, The (Peck), 51
Roosevelt, Franklin, 190
Roosevelt, Theodore, 190
Rose, Calvin Lee, 63–64
Rosenblatt, Mel, 156
Rule changing, 101, 109–14
   and discipline, 115–16
     and managing investments, 116–17
     in reading, 116
   examples of innovators, 103–9
   in business, 103
   and independence, 102–3
   and optimism, 114–15

St. Francis of Assisi, 201–2
Sea Pines Real estate Company, 70–72
Seligman, Martin, 50
Selling, and EPOD solutions, 121–24, 132–35. ACID Test, the; Power Statements
Shaw, George Bernard, 198
Siegel, Bernie, 25, 237
Skaggs-Walsh, 78
Sloan, Alfred, 148
Smith, Fred, 104
Smith, Tom, 104
Smith, Wilson, 104
Studnicky, Jack, 125

Temo, Inc., 57–59
Toastmasters International, 179–80
Townsend, E. Dudley, 173

U.S. Home Systems, 109

Vitale, Giovanni (Nino), 56–59

Wal-Mart, 12–13
Walton, Sam, 13
Wards Company, 105
Webb, Spud, 101–2
Westheimer, Ruth, 190

Windom, Earl, 21–23
Women in management, 185–87
Wurtzel, Samuel, 105

Yoho, Dave, ix–xi, 9, 31, 43, 121,
    214, 219–22, 227, 245–46
  and dawn gray blend shingling,
    117–18
  and love language, 221–22